PORTFOLIO

THE GAME CHANGERS

Yuvnesh Modi has been working towards bringing disruptive technologies to market for the past eight years. He has worked in India and the US, building technology products ranging from the digitization of mom-and-pop retail stores, artificial intelligence (AI) in enterprise software, and most recently bringing robotics and AI to agriculture. Post his integrated master's degree from IIT Kharagpur, he attained an MBA from Harvard Business School. Outside work, Yuvnesh loves playing pick-up soccer and mentors young high-school and college-goers in their pursuit for a career in technology and entrepreneurship.

Rahul Kumar is an alumnus of IIT Kharagpur, from where he graduated with an integrated master's in mathematics and computing in 2013. He is currently an Indian Forest Service officer of the Jharkhand cadre. He is passionate about nature and wildlife.

Alok Kothari has spent the last ten years in AI, working at research and development organizations across India, the Middle East, Europe and the US. He helped build the natural language understanding backend which powers Apple's AI assistant, Siri. He co-founded a blockchain start-up in a Silicon Valley garage whose cryptocurrency is listed on major exchanges like Binance. Alok is now working on his second start-up in AI and healthcare. In his free time, Alok likes to hike and learn new languages.

THE
GAME
CHANGERS

20 EXTRAORDINARY SUCCESS STORIES OF ENTREPRENEURS FROM IIT KHARAGPUR

YUVNESH MODI, RAHUL KUMAR and ALOK KOTHARI

PORTFOLIO
PENGUIN

An imprint of Penguin Random House

PORTFOLIO

USA | Canada | UK | Ireland | Australia
New Zealand | India | South Africa | China | Singapore

Portfolio is part of the Penguin Random House group of companies
whose addresses can be found at global.penguinrandomhouse.com

Published by Penguin Random House India Pvt. Ltd
4th Floor, Capital Tower 1, MG Road,
Gurugram 122 002, Haryana, India

Penguin
Random House
India

First published by Random House India 2012
Published in Portfolio by Penguin Random House India 2021

10 9 8 7 6 5 4 3 2

ISBN 9788184002737

Typeset in Adobe Garamond by Jojy Philip

Printed at Repro India Limited

www.penguin.co.in

MIX
Paper from
responsible sources
FSC® C047271

This is a legitimate digitally printed version of the book and therefore might not
have certain extra finishing on the cover.

To our parents
who have always supported us in our endeavours

CONTENTS

Contents

FOREWORD

The authors of this wonderful book had invited me to write the foreword for this book, and as a proud alumnus of IIT Kharagpur, I was delighted by the idea. This book is a tribute to the achievements of twenty distinguished alumni. Each of these stories is a remarkable tale of success, entrepreneurship, courage of conviction, and leadership. The sum total of the twenty stories tells an even more remarkable tale of a great institution—IIT Kharagpur—which is celebrating its diamond jubilee this year.

Over the last sixty years, IIT Kharagpur has distinguished itself not only among institutions of excellence in the country but also among the very select peer group of other IITs. What sets IIT Kharagpur apart is that even as it excels in academics, it also emphasizes personality development and leadership qualities. At IIT Kharagpur, learning is a 24×7 process—in the classroom and outside. It produces outstanding engineers, but it also produces mature, socially conscious individuals, entrepreneurs, and potential leaders. The twenty stories in this book are just a sample of thousands of others who owe their success and achievement in life to education at this great institution.

It has been forty years since I graduated from IIT Kharagpur. What I learnt there in my formative years has had a very positive influence on my personality and my outlook on life. I owe a great deal to IIT Kharagpur.

My congratulations to Yuvnesh Modi, Rahul Kumar, and Alok Kothari for the commendable effort and enthusiasm they put into writing this book. They have done a very impressive job, in the best traditions of IIT Kharagpur. I wish them all the best.

Dr Duvvuri Subbarao
Governor
Reserve Bank of India

INTRODUCTION

The Indian Institute of Technology, Kharagpur, the torch bearer of the IITs, has just completed six decades of glorious service to the nation. Befitting the milestone, two of its students, Rahul Kumar and Yuvnesh Modi, and an alumnus, Alok Kothari, have written a beautiful book *The Game Changers: 20 extraordinary success stories of entrepreneurs from IIT Kharagpur.*

Environment is crucial to a student and IIT Kharagpur provides the ideal ecosystem to explore and excel in areas other than academics. Its rich environment builds leadership, encourages students to question received knowledge and traditions. IIT Kharagpur is well known for producing leaders in science and engineering worldwide. Its graduates have made an undeniable impact in the professions of their choice. However, little is known about 'KGPians' who have excelled in other areas to become game changers and have left their mark by making breakthroughs in conventional and social entrepreneurship, literature, culture, and public life.

The twenty alumni discussed in this book are some such sung and unsung heroes who have made a difference to themselves and to society. The book gives a glimpse into their lives and achievements. The attempt is to uniformly represent both seniors and juniors, and throw new light on their lives and their journey to success.

I am sure this path-breaking accomplishment of Yuvnesh Modi, Rahul Kumar, and Alok Kothari will be widely appreciated. This book will be of value to those who wish to traverse untrodden ways and create a niche for themselves.

Dr Damodar Acharya
Director
IIT Kharagpur

THE IDEA

'Here in the place of that Hijli Detention Camp stands the fine monument of India, representing India's urges, India's future in the making. This picture seems to me symbolical of the changes that are coming to India.'

These were the words of India's first Prime Minister, Pandit Jawaharlal Nehru, on the very first convocation of IIT Kharagpur in 1956. Fifty-five years later, IIT has emerged as one of the elite temples of education in the country. Today, after sixty years since its inception, IIT Kharagpur is globally renowned for being the proverbial birthplace of innumerable legends. As three curious students of IIT Kharagpur, we began to question, who are these people who have helped IIT become the brand it is today?

We had a brainstorming session and did a quick search on the famous people to have graduated out of this hallowed institution. We observed something peculiar about the sample set we had come across—apart from being IITians, they didn't have much in common. They all had made a name for themselves in completely different walks of life, sometimes quite different from what they had pursued during their undergraduate years. However, there was another thing which connected them all, the word 'entrepreneur'.

We further attempted to explore the idea of what or who is an entrepreneur and what impact they create on their surroundings. It emerged that at the cusp of the rise of a successful nation or a community there was an entrepreneur or a group of them.

So, how does one define an entrepreneur?

The generic definition which Wikipedia provides is: *An entrepreneur is a person who shifts economic resources out of lower and into higher productivity and greater yield.* This definition is simplistic and means an entrepreneur is an efficient businessman, who is able to make monetary profits. However, when one looks at some of the entrepreneurs, the likes of Dr Harish Hande, monetary profits was not their ultimate aim of doing the things they did. So we asked ourselves, what exactly makes a person an entrepreneur. Is it being a businessman, or an inventor, or a social activist?

None of the definitions we came across could successfully be applied to all the entrepreneurs we learnt about. All the people we shortlisted were described by the same umbrella word, yet they were so different from each other in what they did.

There was only one solution to our dilemma—to meet them and learn about their journey to success. We desired to learn what made them do the things they did. Moreover, what were the challenges or impediments they faced when they chose to walk on the path of entrepreneurship and how did they overcome them. We didn't want to limit these experiences to ourselves but share it with a multitude of people. Hence, we hit upon the idea of writing a book about these individual experiences.

Our aim was to interview a set of entrepreneurs who were as diverse as possible. The motive was to get a perspective of the extent to which the spectrum of entrepreneurship can be stretched. We interviewed entrepreneurs like Arjun Malhotra, who was at the forefront of the IT revolution in India, to social activists like Arvind Kejriwal. Entrepreneurs like Dr Suhas Patil and Vinod Gupta, who successfully started up their ventures abroad and explored opportunities in the US, provided us with a more global outlook. Whereas stories of entrepreneurs like Vijay Kumar, who breathed life into an ailing industry, were fascinating to hear about. Lastly, there were those like Sam Dalal, who had the guts to follow their childhood passion and turn it into something larger than life.

It was also important to encompass entrepreneurs from different eras, as the eras presented their own unique problems and constraints. For example, one cannot talk about starting a company in the 1970s and 1980s in India without mentioning how the individuals had to overcome the limitations caused by the draconian Licence Raj. It was also imperative to cover entrepreneurs who have launched their enterprises in the recent past, as their experiences through the initial struggle would be more relevant to people who want to start up now.

We got more than we bargained for. These people were not only successful but were also awe-inspiring personalities. For them it was not about earning a million bucks but about changing a million lives. Often they had to take hard decisions, with a lot at stake. However, they had the vision to look past those difficult times and do what needed to be done. Each entrepreneur was different from the other, yet they shared the same passion for what they did or believed in.

Hence, we finally got our answer—to us, an entrepreneur is a person who stood for what he or she believed in and was able to transform the lives of others through his or her action.

We sincerely hope that our readers enjoy these stories and perhaps get inspired by them. There is something to learn for everybody in this. In the end we all dream big, but it's all about starting small!

Rahul, Alok, and Yuvnesh

AN INDIAN REVOLUTIONARY IN SILICON VALLEY

Dr Suhas Patil

RK Hall, 1965
Cirrus Logic (Founder)

If you're aware of Silicon Valley's rise to global fame, you've definitely heard of a man called Suhas Patil and the company he founded—Cirrus Logic.

What makes Suhas's story so unique is that he was one of the first Indian entrepreneurs in Silicon Valley to succeed. He opened up a whole new territory for other technocrats from India who came to this promised land in hordes to contribute to its ever-growing success. In 1992, in order to help the increasing number of Indians who were starting up, he co-founded The Indus Entrepreneurs (TiE) and became its founding President. His contributions as a mentor to many have placed him on the boards of a number of companies. Even at the ripe old age of 67, he continues to support new and exciting ideas.

AN INDIAN REVOLUTIONARY IN
SILICON VALLEY

Dr Suhas Patil

IN THE YEAR 1995, the Santa Clara Valley Historical Association published a book titled *The Making of Silicon Valley: A One Hundred Year Renaissance,* in which it named Suhas Patil's company Cirrus Logic as one of the companies that shaped the Valley. The book went on to say that '[**Cirrus Logic] rocketed…to a billion-dollar-a-year run rate faster than any other Silicon Valley semiconductor firm ever made that climb—and without a fab of its own.**'

Suhas's earliest encounters with technology, especially electronics, were shaped by his father—his first teacher, and took place while growing up in the steel city of Jamshedpur in Jharkhand. Suhas says his father was a man with multiple skills. He was the first ever engineer from his village, where not even a high school existed. He studied both mechanical and electrical engineering from Banaras Hindu University (BHU) but joined as a metallurgist in TISCO (now called Tata Steel). If that was not enough, he moved to the cost accounting department and ended up as the Chief Financial Officer of the company.

Suhas's father, in order to support his brother and sister through college, had opened a radio repair shop as a side business. Young Suhas spent many hours in the shop playing with radios and other tools strewn about the place. So, he learnt how to fix equipment very early in life. He even made a small radio transmitter by reading *Radio Amateur's Handbook*, published by the American Radio Relay League.

Pursuing his love for electronics, Suhas joined the Department of Electronics and Electrical Communication Engineering, IIT Kharagpur, in 1960. During those days electronics was a new field of study, and it was not the most popular course to choose if you wanted a job with a big salary. However, for Suhas, the option of studying something else did not exist. The department was relatively small with only twelve students in his batch. However, it had an outstanding faculty with professors such as G.S. Sanyal, J. Das, and B. Chatterjee who had studied abroad and were very highly regarded.

Suhas had his fair share of fun while studying at IIT. He was the gardening secretary of RK Hall, which he says was a much respected position. There were almost a hundred flower beds in the garden. Occasionally on Sundays, Suhas would gather all his hall mates and they'd go about planting seedlings in the flower beds. It was done with enthusiasm and during his leadership, his hall never failed to win the trophy for the best garden on campus.

In addition to being the gardening secretary, Suhas was an avid photographer. He learnt photography from his father and gradually mastered all the techniques. '**I distinctly remember an incident when Padmaja Naidu, daughter of Sarojini Naidu and the then Governor of West Bengal, came to inaugurate the Sarojini Naidu Hall [the girls' hostel], and** the official cameraman went missing in action. So, I was asked to take the photographs with my camera.' That black-and-white photograph can still be found adorning the wall of Sarojini Naidu Hall.

While at IIT, Suhas learnt of the great institution, Massachusetts Institute of Technology (MIT), and he was intrigued by the idea of studying there. Graduating as a department topper in 1965, he applied for a postgraduate degree to MIT and got selected. He also got a teaching assistantship, without which he wouldn't have been able to afford his studies.

Coming to MIT in 1965, he was a teaching assistant to the legendary Professor Amar Bose—the maker of the renowned Bose speaker systems. Then Professor Bose was also running Bose Corporation, a company which subsequently put him on the Forbes billionaires list. Suhas's IIT education ensured a smooth sailing for him at MIT. He thoroughly enjoyed every minute of his time at MIT and loved the teamwork between faculty members who were also some of the best researchers he had ever met.

At MIT, in 1966, Suhas created the first ever online information management system in the world. It was during that summer Suhas landed a job at MIT for writing software for the management of teaching and research assignments. He could have written a complete thesis on the project. However, since he had a strong engineering background, he wanted to work in the field of computer architecture.

Suhas's dedication and hard work paid off. In recognition of his outstanding work as a teaching assistant, he was appointed as an instructor even before he finished his doctorate. After he received his Doctor of Science (DSc) degree in Electrical Engineering in 1970, he was immediately invited to join the faculty at MIT.

Suhas began his career as Assistant Professor, and served as Assistant Director of Project MAC (Multi-Access Computer) as well. MAC was a very strong programme, from which things like Ethernet—the predecessor of the Internet— emerged. Project MAC formed a big part of Suhas's doctoral thesis. While working closely with Project MAC, he became interested in semiconductors and methodology of design. Day-by-day, the number of transistors on new chips was increasing and designing those chips was becoming difficult.

Suhas got married and in no time his first child was ready for school. He felt it was time to return to his homeland. He came to India in 1974 and enquired at a very famous electronics company, whose head, on a visit to MIT, had extended Suhas an invitation to join the company. On finding a number of friends from IIT at the company, Suhas thought it was the perfect place to work in. However, the attitude of people at higher positions was hostile; they felt that their own jobs would be at risk if people like Suhas joined the company. Dissatisfied, he enquired at another company which was building computers. The company wanted him to copy the existing models of a computer rather than build one from scratch. After a rich exposure to new technologies in the US, Suhas felt disillusioned with the prospect of not using his experience to the fullest. He knew he had the ability to build the next generation of machines if there was a requirement for them. Disheartened, he returned to MIT.

In 1975, Suhas moved to the University of Utah as it had a semiconductor lab donated to it by General Instrument Corporation (GIC). Suhas completed his work on methodology of design, which came to be known as Storage Logic Array (SLA) methodology. He even made a practical silicon compiler in 1980. He felt that the technology was mature enough to be introduced in the market. However, the methodology that he had developed was a complete departure from the standard methodology, so it was very difficult for the industry to adopt it. The sponsoring company, GIC, funded him to commercialize the technology as it wanted to build a system on a chip.

Suhas's transformation from a professor to an entrepreneur had begun. He quit his job at the University of Utah. GIC invited him to join the company. But Suhas wanted to work independently to which the company agreed. This led him to start a company called Patil Systems in 1981 in Salt Lake City, Utah. The company got a two-year contract from GIC to make commercially viable silicon compilers.

Suhas received full support from his family for this idea. His father, who had retired from TISCO, came to Utah and assisted with the accounting operations, and Suhas's siblings were also very encouraging.

The transition from an academic life to the hustle and bustle of an entrepreneur's was not a smooth one for Suhas. 'It **was very difficult for me as I had no background in finance nor had anyone in my family run an independent business. Business was a whole new world for me. It was a real-time, intense learning experience for me, something like the second year in IIT,**' he says. Suhas used to attend talks by successful entrepreneurs when he was at the university. The notes he'd taken and tips he'd absorbed came in handy now.

However, things didn't unfurl as Suhas thought they would. In early 1983, the company bagged a contract from the cable television division of GIC to design a single-chip solution, and a letter of intent to manufacture 300,000 units of chips for cable set-top boxes at $4 each. Suhas's company designed the chip for the set-top boxes in just four months but it had no money for manufacturing them. After a lot of thought, Suhas concluded that it would be better for him to give away his precious design to someone who could make it for the customer so that there would at least be proof that his novel methodology worked. The semiconductor division of GIC was willing to take the design and make the chips to meet the needs of the customer. He wasn't paid any money upfront or any royalty either. Many years later Suhas still has no regrets about his move. '**When you are at the top of an organization, you quickly find out what a lonely place it is to be in when it comes to making tough decisions. The well being of your employees and their families is at stake. It requires careful** thought; you can talk to your advisers but at the end you have to take the decision on your own. I have never regretted that decision to give away the design,' he says.

But nothing moved in spite of giving away the design till late 1983. So, he called the CEO of GIC, a billion-dollar corporation, and said, 'I have to see you, I absolutely have to see you.' Because of the strength of his conviction, the CEO agreed to meet him. At the meeting, Suhas convinced the CEO to ask his semiconductor division to process the chip, otherwise he would not know whether his design methodology worked or not. At the end of the meeting the CEO told Suhas that he would review the progress of the project. And just like that the chip was processed in a record time of twenty-one days! The chip worked flawlessly and this would subsequently prove to be a giant step in the progress of the company.

The going was tough. Suhas gradually came to the realization that getting business in Utah was difficult. Most of his potential customers were based either in the East or the West Coast, and he did not have access to the venture capital funds available in Silicon Valley. It was during the Christmas holidays in late 1983 that Suhas and his team packed their bags and decided to relocate to Silicon Valley, California. 'I had seven employees—all of whom were my students—out of which only three came with me at that point of time. However, in about a year, all of them came back, and we were together again,' he says with a smile.

In Silicon Valley, Suhas met Michael Hackworth, Senior Vice President of Signetics Corp., Inc., the Silicon Valley based semiconductor subsidiary of the North American division of Philips, and a former marketing executive for Fairchild Industries and Motorola. Suhas thought Hackworth, with his marketing and management experience, might be the perfect complement to him. Hackworth left Signetics to join Patil Systems as the President and CEO, while Suhas assumed the title of Chairman and Executive Vice President Products and Technology. Fred Nazem, a well known venture capitalist (VC), provided the venture capital for the company, and in 1984, it was renamed Cirrus Logic. Cirrus clouds are the highest clouds in the sky; the team believed that the name would provide an accurate representation of the sophistication of their products.

The first major chip manufactured by Cirrus Logic was for set-top converters, the design for which Suhas had already given away to GIC.

When Suhas had relocated to Silicon Valley, GIC asked him to design an improved version of the chip. Suhas says, **'Only my team knew how to improve the design, so GIC got back to us. That was an important learning lesson.'** This time Cirrus had money and manufactured the chip using other companies' chip fabrication facilities. Fabrication is the process used to create the integrated circuits that are present in everyday electrical and electronic devices. Cirrus sold 4 million units of that chip and that was the first time it earned a million dollars in just one quarter.

Suhas had struck gold. This novel business model revolutionized the chip design industry. He knew that the semiconductor technology had matured into a level where one could design chips by using other people's fabrications and attend to the variations of design automation. That in effect was a 'fabless' (fabrication-less) model of doing business. Earlier semiconductor companies worked on both design and fabrications. Setting up fabrication facilities was a very costly affair. Cirrus Logic became the first company to successfully practise the fabless model. Suhas is still proud that he created this model of chip designing, and it remains the industry standard even now.

With the personal computer (PC) boom in the mid-1980s, Cirrus's innovations eventually led to the creation of more compact hard drives.

Cirrus then forayed into graphics- and communication-related products. When IBM unveiled Video Graphics Array (VGA) in 1987 as the new standard for graphics display, Cirrus easily bested others in producing the first fully compatible VGA controller microchip.

Cirrus became one of the biggest success stories of Silicon Valley. In 1989, the company went public, with a valuation of over $150 million. The cash raised by the initial public offering (IPO) helped Cirrus acquire a string of companies to broaden its technical expertise. From 1990 to 1993, Cirrus acquired four companies. In 1993, the company announced that it would produce customized microchips for Apple's Newton personal digital assistant.

The company touched a revenue figure of $1 billion in 1994. '**Every PC had at least one chip from Cirrus Logic**,' Suhas proudly claimed at that time.

In 1997, Suhas stepped down from the management of Cirrus Logic and now holds the position of Chairman Emeritus. He is the Chairman and CEO of Cradle Technologies, a company that makes advanced networked video surveillance products. It was spun off from Cirrus in 1998 to focus on bringing in the next major change in the semiconductor industry and Suhas is relentlessly working towards that goal.

SUHAS'S ACHIEVEMENTS

Suhas is the recipient of several patents in the field of integrated circuits and has published over forty scientific papers. He has served on the board of the Computer History Museum, the Tech Museum, and the World Affairs Council of Northern California. He was the first person to receive the Entrepreneurial Achievement Award from PanIIT in 2009.

An honorary DSc degree was conferred upon him, along with Dr A.P.J. Abdul Kalam who later became the President of India, by IIT Kharagpur in 1995. This made him the first IIT alumnus to receive an honorary doctorate from the IITs. He was declared a Life Fellow of the institute in 2002.

The success of Cirrus inspired other Indians in Silicon Valley to start their own companies. Suhas the mentor of Cirrus was in huge demand. He has always patronized minds. 'I distinctly remember meeting Sabeer Bhatia at a forum after he had graduated from Stanford University. He talked about free email. I was curious and asked him how he would make money. After he explained it, I knew that he was bang on target. It was a great idea. As we know, Hotmail was bought by Microsoft because of the power of its reach,' he says.

By the early 1990s, a host of Indians had become successful in Silicon Valley and they desired to give back to society. In late 1992, they met at the Hilton San Jose Hotel and decided to meet there every month over dinner to figure out the best possible way to contribute. In about a year, they came up with a solution—transmit the knowledge of building companies to the next generation of entrepreneurs in a systematic way. Thus, The Indus Entrepreneurs (TiE) was born. Suhas was its founding President. Other people joined gradually. 'When you are highly visible it's difficult to track people and build an organization, many people told me. It was a challenge which I readily accepted.'

In May 1994, when TiE planned its first TiE Conference, now known as TiECon, Suhas expected less than three hundred people. However, the event was a smashing success, with an attendance of 500 people. There was no looking back, and today TiE brand has become globally synonymous with entrepreneurship. This non-profit organization has a presence in more than fifty-seven locations spread over fourteen countries.

Suhas had not forgotten the years spent at IIT even after many years abroad. As the golden jubilee of IIT Kharagpur was approaching in 2001, Suhas wanted to do something for his alma mater. Those were the early days of Internet and Professor Sanyal and the Director of the institute had approached him with the idea of building kiosks inside the institute campus for students to access the Internet. Suhas knew that the Internet was going to become an integral part of learning in the future. He argued that such a powerful tool should be accessible in each student's room. So, instead of donating money for a building, he was willing to place the institute on the Internet superhighway. The campuswide Internet is his and Arjun Malhotra's gift to their alma mater. The $5.9 million Internet connectivity project has given a huge boost to IIT Kharagpur. It was one of the first campuses in the country to have a campuswide network, all due to Suhas. He also played a key role in the establishment of the advanced Very Large Scale Integration (VLSI) laboratory in the institute. To his other alma mater, MIT, Suhas donated $1.5 million for the construction of the Suhas and Jayashree Patil Conference Center at the Stata Center.

Suhas doesn't shirk from the responsibility of being a role model. He feels it's his duty to inspire people. That's why he finds himself on the boards of a number of companies, both in Silicon Valley and in India. He says, '**I am on the boards of small companies. It doesn't mean that I run the companies; I can only guide them. I am mostly involved in** product-based companies. In such companies you have to create a beautiful product. If it fails in the market, then you have to quickly switch gears. Young people have a better understanding of the current markets and I find it really exciting to work with them.'

During his early days with Patil Systems, Suhas learnt two important practical lessons from his mentor, Mr Larry Hills, Senior Vice President at GIC. First, control the cost you are incurring by controlling the number of employees. Always hire only when you absolutely need someone, so that you don't add numbers unnecessarily. Second, write a report at the end of each month so that you can take stock, and there is no confusion about whether the team is progressing on the right path.

Suhas advocates an academic route to those who want to have a company based on technology. 'Do a PhD, as it is not easy to accomplish. Along the way, you will learn some vital lessons which will be helpful in your entrepreneurial life. The doctoral thesis is an uncharted territory. The professor is your guide and is not feeding you ready-made material. The PhD also teaches you how to manage your emotions, disappointments, and difficulties. An academic life teaches you many small and important things. For example, at IIT, I learnt about issues of labour during a boring Economics class. Today, I value those lessons which, back then, seemed to be unimportant. If you take your studies seriously, then it will bring out the best in you.'

Suhas has the utmost respect for the people who stayed behind in India and helped it reach where it is today. However, he is concerned about the quality and attitude of technologists the country is producing at the moment. **'I sincerely think that engineers are more worried about looking for managerial jobs than their studies. They are losing their competency as engineers as compared with the rest of the world. Even the institutes are not able to retain quality faculties. If these factors are not rectified soon, India will fall behind.'** He wants to see an India which is known not just as the best but also as doing the best.

Suhas is a person who, despite being a legend in the IIT community and Silicon Valley, maintains a very low profile. **'It's very much an Indian character trait that you work hard and you will be recognized. When I became rich I didn't go and buy fancy cars, I bought safe cars which were not second-hand!'** The soft-spoken academic-at-heart, adds, **'People will give you credit if you have done something good!'**

SUHAS'S SUCCESS TIPS

- Follow your passion, not the latest fashion. If you want to be an entrepreneur or achieve greatness in whichever field you work, you need to be fascinated by something. Without fascination, it is difficult to muster the strength to achieve something.

- Realize what you are good at. Then work really hard to achieve success. You should thoroughly explore the field and see what's there for you.

- Have focus and the desire to apply yourself and learn fast and survive. Then you'll succeed. Once you succeed, then you can build on that.

- Be patient. Don't be hasty in taking big decisions.

- Never think that you have lost an opportunity; there will be plenty coming your way.

SAILING AGAINST THE TIDE

Vijay Kumar

RP Hall, 1966
Bharati Shipyard (Co-founder)

Vijay Kumar is the perfect example of the generation hailed as 'Nehru's Children'. In 1973, Vijay, along with his batchmate, P.C. Kapoor, established Bharati Shipyard—a first-of-its-kind company which can be credited for changing the face of the shipbuilding industry in India.

In 2004, Bharati Shipyard became the first private shipyard in India to go public.

'SHRIVASTAV BHUKHA MAREGA' was the running joke at IIT about the choice of Vijay's course. Vijay had chosen Naval Architecture as a discipline, and back in the 1960s, it was generally thought that there were very limited opportunities for naval architects. Hence the joke that he (Shrivastav being his surname) would die hungry.

Vijay and his friends often found themselves wondering if they should drop a year and try for a fancier course like Mechanical Engineering the following year. He had had the option of studying Mechanical Engineering at IIT Bombay but he had never considered it. For him, IIT Kharagpur was the best in the country.

His decision proved to be a prudent one for two reasons: first, Vijay was surrounded by some of the best minds in the country at IIT Kharagpur and was greatly influenced by them. As he very clearly puts it, '**Whatever you are or you become is primarily dependent on three things: your genes, what you inherit from your ancestors; second, perseverance, the effort you put into whatever you do; and finally, the environment you live in. IIT Kharagpur provided us with a tremendous environment and the ability to face, analyse, and solve problems. We learnt some of the most important things of life implicitly.**' The second reason was that when

Vijay graduated in 1966, after mechanical engineers, the highest salaries were given to naval architects.

In February 1967, after graduating, Vijay and P.C. Kapoor, his batchmate at IIT and future business partner, joined a public sector shipyard, Mazagon Dock. But in a few months' time they were disillusioned with their jobs. He says, '**Both Mr Kapoor and I felt that more could be done, but we were not allowed to express ourselves. Ours wasn't a dream of starting a big company but of doing something more substantial. We felt that the shipbuilding industry had a lot of potential, which Mazagon Dock was not exploiting.**'

At that point of time, there was a paradigm shift going on in the shipbuilding industry. Due to high labour costs and a lack of competitive edge, shipbuilding was gradually moving from Europe to Asia. The traditional shipbuilding European countries, such as Great Britain, Greece, and the Scandinavian countries, were quickly losing business to Asian countries, mainly Japan and South Korea. However, the Indian shipbuilding industry couldn't leverage this opportunity due to its low capacity, poor productivity, lack of modernization, and stringent international trade policies.

One thing led to another, and soon Vijay and P.C. Kapoor found themselves envisioning their own shipbuilding company. It wasn't a concrete plan, but they knew that the shipbuilding industry in India had a big future ahead of it, and they wanted to be a part of it.

In 1972, Vijay told his parents he wanted to start a company and go into business entirely. His father, who was in a government job with Hindustan Steel Limited (HSL), now known as SAIL, was sceptical of the decision—he wanted Vijay to join the navy or take up a stable government job. But in due time, he came to support Vijay's decision. Unfortunately, both his parents passed away in 1973, the year Vijay started his business. And in 1973, Vijay Kumar and P.C. Kapoor walked out of Mazagon Dock with one month's salary in their pockets, a lot of ignorance, and a big dream to join hands with their friend, Suresh Jagtiani, and start their very own company—Bharati Shipyard.

It would be technically wrong to say Vijay and his partners started the company. Bharati Shipyard already existed as a company. The people who started the company had registered it but couldn't build the shipyard due to certain constraints, and thus were unable to repay their loans. So, Vijay and his partners not only got themselves an already registered company but also the funds to run it, as the bank had transferred the loans from the previous owners to them. Moreover, the previous owners agreed to wait three years to receive the payment due to them. Vijay and his partners started off modestly. They approached the State Bank of India (SBI) for more loans and they got lucky. In the 1970s, Indira Gandhi had started an entrepreneur scheme under which any college graduate wanting to start an enterprise was given Rs 1 lakh as a loan.

Bharati Shipyard secured its first order from the Government of Andhra Pradesh to build five barges. They had quoted the lowest amount for the tender. '**It was a brave decision taken by the then Port Officer, Captain Satyanandam. He knew we had no one to back us if something went wrong. If we ran out of money, the project would suffer and most probably come to a stop, and the Captain was aware that we weren't in a position to secure more funds,**' Vijay recalls. However, the Captain trusted the abilities of the young naval architects. He did lay down some conditions, one being that the construction had to be done in his own port in Kakinada, so that if anything went wrong he would have the work done till then available to him.

Bharati Shipyard delivered its first ship in 1975. It was a proud moment for the fledgling start-up. The government was satisfied with the product, and by 1977 the order for all the vessels was completed.

Word soon spread about Bharati Shipyard, bagging it many orders at Ratnagiri. But it was still in uncharted waters, and the going was anything but smooth. Vijay and his friends, being in their late twenties, found it difficult to convince clients about their capabilities. Others couldn't believe that people so young could run a business of their own. It was very challenging, but being young, they didn't take the general scepticism about them too seriously, and took risks and decisions without much worry.

Bharati Shipyard sailed through the 1970s without any major storm ruffling its masts, but at the same time without any major achievement catapulting its turnover. Its first huge opportunity to increase revenue came in the form of a business proposal worth Rs 20 to 25 crore. Vijay and his team believed that they could pull the deal off; however, they required a bank guarantee to clinch it. The bankers were anxious about the proposal as it would multiply the company's credit limit by ten times. Vijay took a leap of faith and told the bank that Bharati Shipyard would do the work and that the clients would pay the bank instead, in return for the bank guarantee. And once the bank was confident of Bharati Shipyard executing the deal, it could start giving them the money. Vijay's ingenuity paid off; Bharati Shipyard gained the bank guarantee and was eventually able to increase its turnover tenfold.

After its successful start, Bharati Shipyard hit a slump in 1979–80; a slump which taught Vijay and his colleagues many vital lessons about the industry. The global shipbuilding industry was going through a recession and there was no work in the market. No matter how hard it tried, Bharati Shipyard couldn't bag any orders. It came to realize that the shipbuilding trade is cyclic in nature. The slump soon petered out and by 1981–82, it was back in business. This cycle, the profitable one, that is, lasted for about ten to twelve years, and it was during this time that Bharati Shipyard received its first order from Europe. However, in 2000, it once again faced a massive slump, and it brought with it a host of other problems. By 2002, Bharati Shipyard was in serious trouble.

THE LICENCE RAJ

After Independence and until 1990, it was mandatory for companies to obtain complex licences. This was commonly referred to as the Licence Raj. For a long time after India gained Independence, its economic policy was governed by the colonial government that had ruled it, which most Indian leaders felt was an unfair practice. The policy's main focus was on protectionism, with a strong emphasis on lesser import, a large public sector, business regulation, and central planning. And all businesses in the 1980s in India had to take into account the demons—Inspector Raj and Licence Raj.

Bharati Shipyard, too, couldn't escape their fangs. One of the biggest problems it faced was acquiring steel at controlled rates. In the first deal at Kakinada it acquired steel by using the essentiality certificate, a relic of the Licence Raj, which was issued by the government. It gave the company to which the certificate was issued special privileges to buy anything essential immediately to complete the job.

The biggest defeat that Bharati Shipyard suffered at the hands of bureaucracy was when it lost out on a deal with Coal India. Theirs was the cheapest quote, but Coal India was not confident of Bharati Shipyard's ability. Vijay, however, pressed on and finally convinced Coal India to give them the tender. It was at this point when the real problems began. A few people at Coal India were not happy that Bharati Shipyard had secured the deal, and came in the way of the company procuring the necessary import licence. Hence, Bharati Shipyard ultimately lost the deal.

It was the worst period in the history of the company and for shipbuilding in general. Even the banks had turned their backs on Bharati Shipyard. The mistake of banking solely with one bank had come back to bite the company. There were new people in SBI who didn't have faith in the company. Vijay and his team were at a loss as to where the money would come from and how they would pay their employees' wages and their suppliers. But, out of the blue, Bharati Shipyard got its lucky break. There was a change in management, and the new bank chairman happened to be the deputy managing director of ten years ago, and he had had faith in Bharati Shipyard. In no time, Bharati Shipyard was granted the loan it so desperately required. Vijay recalls, '**We learnt a very important lesson that time—to never put all our eggs in one basket. SBI is the best bank, but today I don't solely rely on them; I have other banks to fall back on. It's good to be conservative but at times you've got to break the mould and take some risks.**'

If 2000–02 was the trough on the wave to success for Bharati Shipyard, then the year 2004 can be regarded as the point where it started its journey to the crest. The Government of India had passed a legislation conducive for the shipbuilding industry in the Tenth Planning Commission. In December 2004, Bharati Shipyard became the first shipyard to go public, and its issue was oversubscribed 78 times, a record in the Bombay Stock Exchange at that time. Vijay recalls that the oversubscription of shares gave them and the market a lot of confidence. '**We didn't** believe in taking loans, and every time we did, we paid it back as quickly as we could. Maybe that's why our public issue was so successful. We had a billion dollars of oversubscribed money for ten to fifteen days. And for those few days, we felt very, very rich!' It's interesting to know that when the company went public, it had zero debt.

Bharati Shipyard has gone through massive expansion since then. Its business got a major boost when it acquired Great Offshore in 2009. In 2004, it had two shipyards, and by 2010, it had acquired six shipyards—in Kolkata, Mumbai, Dabhol, Ratnagiri, Goa, and Mangalore. In addition to all this, it is planning two more with the Apeejay Group.

Today, Bharati Shipyard is breaking new ground both nationally and globally. It is building a jackup drill ship (used mostly for oil and natural gas drilling), which costs $185 million apiece—the first time such a ship has been built in the country. It is also building an LNG-propelled ship with an intrinsically safe engine room concept—a first in the world for a cargo ship.

Vijay attributes the success of Bharati Shipyard to its highly motivated team, which never gave up even when the going was tough. They never put too much money in building state-of-the-art facilities, and were smart enough to not splurge or borrow too much. Today, 75 percent of the company's orders are exports, mainly to Europe. And this is because of the great foundation laid down by the team which works round the clock.

BHARATI SHIPYARD'S ACHIEVEMENTS

Till 2000, the shipbuilding industry in India, as compared to the rest of the world, was an absolute nonentity. The country was not even getting 0.1 percent of the world order. After no action for over twenty-five years, the government finally began to support the industry. Bharati Shipyard's order book has increased by a whopping 1734 percent in a five-year time frame. India is now the eighth largest shipbuilding nation in the world, taking 1.7 percent share of the world order book.

The other reason for Bharati Shipyard's success is the great partnership between Vijay and P.C. Kapoor. 'People often ask us how we have sustained this partnership for thirty-seven years. The reason is we have complete faith and trust in each other. If Mr Kapoor told me that he was selling the company, I won't ask him why he wants to sell it. I'll just ask him if I have a job tomorrow or not. I'm sure he would give me his reasons for why he is doing what he is doing. Trust of this kind is essential for a stable partnership,' he says.

Vijay believes that shipbuilding is one of the most important industries for a growing economy as it encourages many other downstream industries. Normally, to build a ship one needs over 30,000 parts. All these various parts need to be purchased and assembled together in a manner not very different from that of the automobile industry. Today, the ancillary automobile industry is worth $15 to $20 billion. The shipbuilding industry is capable of a bigger figure than that. Vijay feels that the potential shipbuilding possesses for the growth of the Indian economy has been grossly underestimated. Being a labour-intensive industry, it is ideal for a country like India where labour costs are low. However, after being a part of various working committees of the Planning Commission, he is disgruntled with the experience. 'Today, at the highest level of the government they call shipbuilding a "strategic" industry. However, they do not enact supporting policies.'

When *Business Standard* ranked Vijay Kumar and P.C. Kapoor at 196 in the list of top Indian billionaires, Vijay was unfazed. It's not the money but what he has achieved with the company, and the industry as a whole, that matters the most to him. He says, 'Doing something as challenging as shipbuilding, that too in a severe pre-liberalization India, and succeeding at it is what brings satisfaction. There were times when I felt frustrated but then I'd think about what a 70-year-old shipbuilder from England had once told me. He said, "Young man, shipbuilding is not a business, it is a way of life", and I'd go back to the business of life.'

Vijay's passion for shipbuilding is rock solid. When asked what's next, he says, 'Getting the country to understand the enormous impact this industry can have.'

We can only say Amen to that.

VIJAY'S SUCCESS TIPS

• Know your goals and plan your strategy. Clarity of thought and vision is of utmost importance.

• Give the process a 100 percent. Even if it's the most trivial of things like making your team member a cup of coffee!

• Be compassionate with your partner, clients, and employees. It is an essential quality in a leader.

• At the same time, you must be competitive. The entrepreneur swims in shark-infested waters.

• You can't do things alone. Build a stable team. Nothing succeeds like teamwork.

TRYST WITH DESTINY

Vinod Gupta

RK Hall, 1967
InfoUSA (Founder)

Vinod Gupta grew up in a village in India, armed himself with an IIT degree, and flew to the US with nothing but the shirt on his back. Even the plane ticket was bought from borrowed money. He started his company, InfoUSA, with just $100.

Today, he is a multimillionaire and has committed all his wealth to charity. From the dusty village lanes of Uttar Pradesh to the corridors of power in the US, Vinod's journey can only be called extraordinary.

AS HE POKED AND PLAYED with the dials of a transistor radio that his friend had brought to school, Vinod 'Vin' Gupta had his first crush on technology. And when he learnt that it had come from a land called 'America', his fascination was further fuelled. He was only in Class 7 then, a young boy absorbed in a shiny new toy.

Vin grew up in Rampur Maniharan, a village in the district of Saharanpur in Uttar Pradesh. As a child, he demonstrated an acumen for business and was quick to spot opportunities. In the village, Vin would procure wheat and rice from the local farmers for cheap, husk it, and then sell it in the market, thereby making a small profit. His father, a village doctor, didn't make a lot of money but got penicillin at a very subsidized rate. The medicine the doctors got from the drug companies was cheaper than what the pharmacies got from the wholesellers. Vin would buy penicillin through his father and then sell it to the pharmacies, making a few extra rupees on the way.

Since the village school was only till Class 10, Vin moved to his father's village, Baraut in Meerut. In March 1961, young Vin and his father bumped into his father's friend and his son while on a walk. The friend's son, Sant Sagar Jain, who later went on to becoming Managing Director of Bird & Company in Kolkata, was an alumnus of IIT Kharagpur's first batch. During the conversation, Mr Jain enquired about Vin's plans after he passed Class 12. Vin replied that he would give the College of Engineering in Roorkee a shot. Mr Jain suggested that he try for IIT Kharagpur instead because it was the best engineering college in the country. Vin had no clue where Kharagpur was, but the words stuck with him, and from thereon there was no shaking the idea out of his young head.

Vin appeared for the joint entrance exam in April 1962 and cleared it with a rank of 1197 among the 1200 results declared. He recalls, '**When I went for the interview, I was informed that I had only one choice—Agricultural Engineering at IIT Kharagpur. It was one of the less popular courses back then, but I didn't care so I took it. I came home and told my family. They were so shocked; it was like they had got bitten by a snake!**'

Vin's first week at IIT was an awakening experience. He met people from all over India who spoke different languages and ate different foods. He felt like he was on a different planet. The IIT experience changed him completely.

Having got into IIT, Vin was sure of getting a job that paid about Rs 400 a month, a good amount in those days, and had no ambitions beyond that. However, there was something that caught Vin's attention. The US consulate would often organize functions at the institute, and the participating

American students would bring with them slick, glossy magazines. Vin was addicted to these magazines, especially *Time* and *Life*. '**I used to go through those magazines and be mesmerized by the pictures of beautiful cars and things I had never seen before.**' Once again he was drawn to the US. He decided that he should do his master's from an American university as that was the trend in those days. However, the biggest limitations were his grades, which were not good by any standard as he just managed to make the passing limit. But even though his grades weren't much to write home about, Vin had his fair share of luck of being at the right place at the right time.

At the end of his penultimate year, Vin trudged off to a farm in Chennai for his summer training. The cruel Chennai heat was too much for Vin to bear so he abandoned it midway and returned home. As a penalty, he was asked by his professor to stay back on campus and complete his training during the Durga Puja holidays when everyone else left for home.

It was during these holidays that Vin met Professor Bill Splinter from the University of Nebraska at Lincoln, US. The professor was visiting IIT under the US government's PL 480 Food for Peace programme to solve India's agricultural problems. Vin would take the professor out for drinks and dinner as they were virtually the only ones on campus, and soon they became fast friends. It was on one such occasion that the professor suggested that Vin do his master's in Nebraska. Vin agreed immediately, and sat for his GRE

(Graduate Record Exam). Despite his low score, Vin secured a scholarship because of Professor Splinter.

In August 1967, Vin set foot on American soil with $58 in his pocket and a suitcase of clothes. Coming from a village with no running water, no phones, no electricity, no paved roads, Vin was completely blown away by Lincoln. Vin recalls, **'It even had a map so that I could find my way around!'**

The master's programme at Nebraska was once again an eye-opener. The professors were very good, friendly, and extremely dedicated. On completion of his master's, Vin decided to get an MBA degree too. He got a call from Harvard but he didn't have the tuition money so he enrolled into the MBA programme at Nebraska as it offered him a full-time job too. Vin thoroughly enjoyed the MBA programme, more so because he could also work full time.

While at the University of Nebraska, Vin forayed into a small business of his own to earn some additional money. He imported precious stones from a friend in India and sold them to jewellers in Nebraska. After completing his MBA, Vin got a job at Omaha, Nebraska, as a market research analyst at Commodore Corporation, a mobile home manufacturing company. However, he kept himself busy in his own business as he was not satisfied with the $750 per month salary at Commodore. He gradually moved from jewels to importing carved wooden items.

For the Christmas of 1971, he had ordered $20,000 worth of wooden items at a cost of $10,000. Vin was excited at the prospect of a huge profit margin. However, his consignment reached the seaport only to find that the longshoremen had gone on strike. This ruined all of Vin's efforts as he could not deliver the goods on time and everyone cancelled the orders as they were intended as Christmas presents. In the meantime, he had to give a letter of credit from his bank and then quickly had to sell everything for whatever price he could get. Vin ended up with a debt of $8000. Fortunately, Vin knew the banker well, and told him the entire story. He still remembers the banker's words, '**The fact that you came to me and told me the truth is important, I trust you. You can take as long as you want to repay it.**' Vin learnt an important lesson that day, one that he'd never falter on—be truthful with your bank!

At Commodore Corporation, there was a need for a list of mobile home dealers for the salespeople in the company. Vin bought the list from Dun & Bradstreet, but it wasn't very accurate. Realizing that the $3000 list was useless, his infuriated boss asked him to find a solution. He told his boss that they could get the list from the yellow pages, the telephone directories of businesses, published by AT&T, a telecom company. Vin rang up the telecom company and enquired about the cost of all the yellow pages books for the whole country. After two months, the phone company informed him that the cost of the 4800 yellow pages books for the whole country would be $8000. Vin declined the offer as Commodore couldn't afford it. A couple of months later, the phone company asked him if Commodore had an 1800 toll-free line. When Vin said that it did, the phone company offered the phone books for free! It was trying to promote the use of long distance calls. It was a lucky accident and Vin readily accepted the offer.

One day, three months later, Vin came to the office and found his boss in the reception area surrounded by a mountain of boxes filled with phone books, fuming. '**He yelled at me, "Gupta, get those damn boxes out of here by 4 pm, otherwise I am going to fire you"**,' Vin recalls with a grin. Vin called a local trucking company and it hauled all the books to his garage at home. Now Vin had a garage full of phone books and an angry wife. He opened all the boxes and arranged all the books on the floor state-wise. The next day, Vin went and told his boss that creating the list would take a long time and involve expenses because somebody had to go through all the books and sort out the names, addresses, and zip codes of the dealers. His boss asked him how much it would cost, and Vin gave him an approximate figure of $10,000. Commodore didn't want to spend so much money. A natural entrepreneur, Vin offered him an alternative, '**If I can sell this list to the company's competitors and make money, you can have it free of cost.**' His boss happily opted for the latter. This simple and smart idea put Vin on a path from which he has never looked back.

Vin went through the books and made a sample list of around 300 names of dealers of a particular state and got it printed. He sent out the sample along with a brochure and a letter to a 1000 manufacturers saying he had this wonderful list of mobile home dealers priced at 10 cents a name. It cost him $100, which he borrowed from the same bank he always banked with. Vin was basically selling a product without having it. That's what you call the ultimate sell. '**I thought that if there was a market, I would create the product and if there wasn't, then there won't be much money lost.**'

In about eight weeks Vin got orders of $22,000 and $13,000 in cheques as advance money. There was a huge demand for the lists. To cover the cost of compiling the lists, Vin used the advance money he received. Vin and his wife wrote out all these names and had them key punched. He also had to hire a lot of part-time people to complete the orders. In about three months, they had the lists ready and printed, and sent out all the orders. In that first year, Vin made a profit of $28,000. The first thing Vin did with that money was to clear his bank debt.

In 1973, the mobile home company that he was working at ran into a host of problems and Vin was laid off. As with earlier accidents, this turned out to be good for him as he could concentrate on his business full time. The turnover went up to $66,000 in that year and then to $100,000. Vin didn't make too much money for himself or his family since the business had huge expenses. To augment his income, he took up a day job in Omaha. On realizing that the sales were not growing much after this shift, Vin had to make up his mind—to close the business or work at it full time. It was a tough decision, but in 1976, he decided to quit his job and focus on growing his business. His revenue grew from $110,000 to $200,000 that year, and he made a profit of $35,000.

In 1977, when the revenue grew to $350,000, Vin started diversifying. Besides mobile home dealers, he created lists for trailer dealers, motorcycle dealers, bicycle dealers, etc., all from the same yellow pages. That year he made a profit of $100,000. It was a lot of money and Vin realized that he finally had a viable business. By 1981, he reached the million-dollar mark in revenue and by 1986 he had covered all businesses in the yellow pages and had a revenue of $9 million.

Soon the business took on a life of its own. It had more employees, its very own building, and was focusing on the quality of its lists by calling each business, verifying their existence, their addresses, and adding other such details. Its area of specialization was transforming from a yellow pages based business to a database business. In 1993, the business had grown to $44 million and the company had acquired two smaller companies in similar areas of work. The company then went public. Vin, at that time, could foresee this becoming a billion-dollar business.

By 1998, the company had undergone many changes and its name was changed to InfoUSA from American Business Information as it was no longer just a business database company. The company had expanded its database to include 11 million US and Canadian businesses, as wells as a consumer database of 113 million households, and had also added database marketing services. The Internet era made information delivery a lot easier. As technology changed, the company adapted to new ways of delivering information—floppies, CDs, and then online access.

Vin then launched a company named Salesgenie in 2003, which sold database as a service through online subscriptions. For instance, customers who usually came once in two to three years for buying a new list of jewellers in a particular city were offered online access to the list at a much lesser monthly charge. Then InfoUSA bought a market research company called Opinion Research in 2006.

INFOUSA'S ACHIEVEMENTS

After the dotcom bubble burst at the beginning of the new millennium, the company bought four email marketing companies worth between $4 million and $6 million; whose market cap had been over $1 billion before the crash. InfoUSA merged these companies and emerged as the largest email deployment company.

Since going public, InfoUSA had made forty-five acquisitions by 2008. The company preferred to make an acquisition only when the management came along with it. It wouldn't change the names of the acquired companies and only provided tools to make them more efficient and profitable. 'It's a mistake to try to change the management or put your own person to manage

---

the business,' says Vin. In June 2008, InfoUSA was renamed InfoGROUP to reflect its global expansion. It was sold in July 2010 for nearly $650 million. The company, at that time, had over 3000 employees across nine countries. Its data powered the top five internet search engines and 90 percent of the GPS deployments in North America.

After InfoGROUP was sold, Vin launched a series of entrepreneurial ventures. He set up expresscopy.com, a company that offers online digital printing services. He also set up Database101.com, a company that provides databases and technology to salespeople and small businesses. His venture infofree.com aims to help salespeople and small business owners to find more customers and grow their sales. His private equity firm, Everest Group, formed in 1987, invests in the business information and marketing information sectors.

VINOD'S ACHIEVEMENTS

Vinod was awarded honorary doctorates from Monterey Institute of International Studies, University of Nebraska, and IIT Kharagpur.

During his presidency, Bill Clinton nominated and confirmed him the US Consul General to Bermuda and US Ambassador to Fiji. Due to business commitments, he declined both times. Clinton appointed him member of the board of trustees of the prestigious John F. Kennedy Center for Performing Arts in Washington, DC. He was declared a Life Fellow of IIT Kharagpur in 2002.

His long road to success, however, has not changed Vin. He says, 'My philosophy is that we come into this world with nothing and we leave with nothing. After I die, everything will go to charity. I believe that the wealth should be given away to the society that gave it to us.' He created the Vinod Gupta Charitable Foundation for his charitable activities.

Vin recognizes the value of education and how it has changed his own life. Through a personal endowment of $2 million in 1991, he set up the Vinod Gupta School of Management at IIT Kharagpur. The school is the foremost B-School in the IIT system. Vin's donation made him a hero and woke up the IIT alumni to the fact that they should do something for their alma mater. 'After my parents, IIT Kharagpur had the biggest influence on my life. I will forever be indebted to this holy place! Going to IIT Kharagpur is like going home. I feel like I know every inch of that soil. Hindus go to Rishikesh for pilgrimage, Muslims go to Mecca, and Christians go to Jerusalem to pray. I just go to IIT Kharagpur,' he says.

It can be said that Vin made 'giving back' fashionable. To meet the demand for intellectual property attorneys, who are well versed in patents and related issues, Vin set up the Rajiv Gandhi School of Intellectual Property Law at IIT Kharagpur in 2006 through an endowment of over $2 million. His idea is that IITs should not be limited to technical education; rather they should offer more curriculums and even impart leadership skills.

Vin's donations in the US include $2 million to establish a curriculum for small business management at the University of Nebraska. He also donated an additional $500,000 to the university to set up a scholarship fund for minority students who want to enter its science or engineering schools.

In 2007, Vin set up the Dr Giri Lal Gupta School for Public Health, named after his father, at the University of Lucknow. It is interesting to know that Vin's father studied medicine at the university along with the former President of India, S.D. Sharma. Mr Sharma, during his presidency, had inaugurated the Vinod Gupta School of Management at IIT Kharagpur in 1994. In the former president's honour, Vin established the Dr Shankar Dayal Sharma Institute of Democracy at the University of Lucknow in 2008.

He says, 'I grew up in a village where there was no school for girls. The girls simply got married and had kids. My mother always wanted a school so that girls could get an education and find meaningful jobs.' And in the year 2000, Vin donated $1 million to set up the Shrimati Ram Rati Gupta Women's Polytechnic, named after his mother, in his village to impart vocational education to girls after their high school education.

In the US, Vin befriended on of its most loved and powerful man—Bill Clinton. Vin's friendship with Bill Clinton has its genesis in an interesting incident in the year 1996. Just before Clinton's presidential re-election, there was a fundraiser at Washington, DC. It was a dinner for people who wanted to contribute to the Democratic Party. Being a Democrat himself, Vin attended the event. Clinton was sitting across him. Vin couldn't help himself and went on to have a long-drawn-out conversation with Clinton. '**I asked him a lot of questions, especially about India and Pakistan. I chided him for favouring China over India. I pointed out to him that China was a very monolithic society and he had already been there two to three times before, but had never been to India, even though India was the world's largest democracy. I teased him that it was unfortunate that the American Presidents prefer dictatorships.**'

Clinton was a little taken aback and invited Vin to the White House. Vin helped him in his re-election campaign and fundraising. They became close friends and even played golf and cards together. Clinton became a consultant for InfoUSA in 2001. In his book *Giving: How Each of Us Can Change the World*, Clinton praises Vin and InfoUSA for their charitable activities.

In April 2001, shortly after Clinton had left the White House, Vin persuaded Clinton to visit his village. Clinton dedicated the Hillary Rodham Clinton Center for Mass Communication to the village. The Center provides training to women in journalism. Clinton also inaugurated the William Jefferson Clinton Science and Technology Center in the village. The Center forms the new science block at Vin's former school. Even though the village lacked an all-weather road and daily electricity supply was limited to just three hours, Clinton was captivated by it.

Vin's vision has been inspired by the idea advocated by Mahatma Gandhi, 'Be the change you want to see in the world.'

VINOD'S SUCCESS TIPS

- The most important and basic thing is to learn and understand the needs of a customer. If the need is fairly large and you can fulfil it, that is the start of an enterprise.

- There is no substitute for passion. It is the road to success. Everything else will fall into place. But first, you've got to want to do the job.

THE ILLUSIONIST

Sam Dalal

RK Hall, 1968
Funtime Innovations (Founder and Head)

Although he no longer dons a magician's robe, he knows the secrets of transporting the audience into a world of illusions. Sam Dalal transformed his childhood hobby of magic into a lucrative business. A pioneering innovator, Sam has taught the world the true meaning of entrepreneurship—doing what you love.

Funtime Innovations is the biggest supplier of self-created products to magicians around the world. Based in Kolkata, the company offers a range of over 1,500 products including magic tricks, books, and props.

'LOOK, THIS IS MY LATEST PRODUCT—"Entanglement"— based on Quantum Entanglement that you study in Quantum Physics,' quips a grinning Sam Dalal in his office-cum-'laboratory'. Sam, with his French-cut beard, who is in his sixties, looks much younger. For him, entrepreneurship was a necessity rather than a choice. Born in a Parsi family, Sam lost his father at the age of six and was left to fend for himself.

Chemistry was Sam's first love. From a very young age, chemistry was sheer magic to him. **'It was really astonishing to see milk being formed by, what seemed like, mixing just water together.'** He would carry around his chemistry sets with him all the time. The sets were intended for young children to learn the principles of chemistry in an interesting and fascinating way by being able to conduct experiments at home. They consisted of all the necessary chemicals and apparatus, along with instructions. He recalls that on his eighth birthday, his mother had given him Rs 5, with which he promptly went out to buy himself the number 1 set of chemistry—a far superior set than his number 0 set, which was the most basic chemistry set. However, the shopkeeper didn't have what Sam was looking for and showed him something else, a magic set called the Conjuring Set. Sam bought the Conjuring Set out of fear that his mother would take back the money if he didn't buy something with it. And in no time, Sam the magician was born.

'At that age you want to learn anything and everything. And I chose magic. For showing five tricks I used to charge 1 anna, which is 1/16th of a rupee. This hobby was an easy way to earn pocket money.' Sam often performed his tricks at school, and even the Rotary Club invited little Sam for a performance.

In 1963, Sam left his little hill station town of Devlali in Maharashtra for IIT Kharagpur to pursue Civil Engineering. Even at IIT, Sam's magic had everyone spellbound. Once, during a ragging session, Sam was asked to perform the William Tell act. 'On the stage, I had a gun in my hand and a guy with a balloon over his head stood at a distance while I was blindfolded. The other boys made a circle around us and were shouting and booing. I loaded the gun and fired a shot. Pin-drop silence followed. I fired another shot and burst the balloon. The jeering stopped. They were all stunned.' Sam also remembers eating glass and razor blades. 'I knew how to do those tricks comfortably. I made fun of the seniors by challenging them to do the same. Ragging became fun for me!' Sam's magic shows were so popular that he was asked to perform at the Annual Hall [hostel] Day every year and was even sent as the sole representative for an inter-IIT function.

Sam used to hold magic shows in Kolkata once a month on weekends. The city, 120 km from Kharagpur, was a four-hour ride by train. If he was lucky, he would sometimes make up to Rs 1200 a month, which was a huge amount back in the 1960s. Sam says with a smile, '**I used to feel like a king. Because in those days, you could have a luxurious date with Re 1!**' However, behind the magic shows lay a compulsion. Sam needed about Rs 200 per month to support his studies as his mother couldn't afford it. He had to perform to earn money.

After graduating from IIT in 1968, Sam didn't get a good job offer. Unlike today, IITians back then weren't placed in fancy jobs. Going abroad for higher studies was a lot easier. Sam had no choice but to earn as he had to support his three younger siblings and his mother. He had done his penultimate year's summer internship in Mumbai with Shah Construction Company, the leading builders of skyscrapers back then. As a trainee, he worked on the foundations of the Air India and Indian Express buildings at Nariman Point—one of Mumbai's first skyscrapers. It paid him Rs 250 a month and offered a job with a little higher pay. '**In Mumbai, one couldn't get a decent room on rent for less than Rs 500. I would have had to struggle to support myself, let alone support my family. So I declined the job offer.**'

Sam's maternal uncle had a pharmaceutical business spread over Bengal and Assam, and he asked Sam to join the business. Sam wasn't really interested, but as he didn't have much of a choice, he took it up.

Sam kept at his magic shows in Kolkata, which helped him earn an additional income. He was earning twice as much as his salary in one 15-minute show. Since he was pretty good at it, he could afford to command any price for his shows. At birthday parties, a magician was usually paid Rs 250, but he would charge Rs 500 and get it.

However, gradually Sam started feeling that he was wasting his time with his hobby. He felt like he'd been doing the same thing since he was 8 years old. He wondered why he wasn't doing something more sophisticated now that he was in his twenties. At that time he thought to himself, 'If I am **going to do this when I am thirty it is fine, but what about when I am in my forties and fiftees, what would people say?**' He realized that he needed to do something more than just magic shows.

An incident in 1973 changed the trajectory of his life. **'Once, I was performing before a bunch of college girls at Trincas, a popular restaurant in Calcutta. As a youngster, I think I was trying to show off. I was performing X-Ray Eyes, in which you have to read and write whatever a spectator writes when you are blindfolded. I asked them to write anything. So one girl came and wrote her name, Pamella, in the Greek alphabet, all letters in upper case. I crossed that and said that my name needs to be accentuated, so I wrote my name in capital and her name in lowercase, all in Greek. As an entertainer you were required to do such things. She got so impressed that she kept asking me how I knew, how I could read Greek. I told her that I had learnt it in college.'** To which she remarked, **"Why is a college graduate doing madari tricks here?"'** These words pricked

Sam's heart like a thorn. He realized that there was no scope for a performer in a country like India. Sam the magician went off the scene forever. He has never performed for money after that event.

During his IIT days, Sam used the workshops of the institute for creating his own tricks. At that time he didn't know that one could buy a trick. His lack of awareness about this fact forced him to innovate. **'I remember making a silver floating ball which I used to perform at magic conventions. This was a commercial trick known as Zombie, but I made it with my own method, and it had some advantages over the commercial ones.'**

When he got out of IIT and joined his uncle's business, he subscribed to some international magic magazines. Besides, he also got his tricks published in international magazines such as *Abracadabra* and *Magigram*. They paid him £5 for publishing an idea. Sam published a few hundred articles from 1968 to 1973 in international magazines. It was no mean achievement.

Sam was thrilled yet distressed by the huge success of his tricks published in the magazines. One day somebody wrote to him about a trick that he had published in *Magigram*. The trick was titled Crystal Thought Condenser. It was a clear cube in which a picture appeared based on the refractive properties of the Perspex. The magazine team had manufactured a product for the trick and put it up at a magic convention. A thousand pieces, at £5 each, were sold and they made

£5000! 'They were selling my idea and making £5000 and here I was, getting just £5 for giving the idea away.' Sam considered manufacturing his own products. And this led to the beginning of his entrepreneurial journey, in a field which would hardly be anyone's choice.

Sam's Magic Service was founded in 1973 with just two people—Sam and a relative. They operated from a small room in their house, working through nights and at odd hours to execute the orders. Sam's family members were completely against this business; they couldn't understand what he was doing. The only one who had faith in him was his wife, Sheila. Sam had fallen in love with her while performing a magic show in 1965 at the South Institute in Kharagpur. He was performing a mind-reading trick, and she came up on the stage as an assisting spectator. Sam had apparently read her mind, and everything else is history.

The venture started growing so rapidly that by 1975 Sam left his uncle's business and devoted all his time to his own. This was a high-margin business. His target in those days was to achieve a sales figure of Rs 7000 a month, resulting in a profit of Rs 3500. Notably, salaries in those days used to be Rs 400 to Rs 500.

In 1983, Sam started Electro Fun to reflect the changing nature of the business. He was very interested in electronics and made good use of it, especially discrete electronics such as transistors, amplifiers, light-operated switches, and sound-operated switches. However, today discrete electronics is almost dead and only visible in the form of integrated circuits. Electro Fun was a purely domestic business, while Sam's Magic Service was an export-oriented business.

In 1992, Electro Fun evolved into Funtime Innovations Pvt. Ltd. Sam's staff and suppliers now owned shares of the company. He did this so that they too could have a stake in the company's future and the business would flourish. Sam's concern was with sustaining his ideas rather than just accumulating money.

Funtime Innovations deals in background business for magicians. **'Everything has a background; a movie has a director, a scriptwriter, and many other people. Likewise, for any magician performing, somebody behind the curtains is doing the creative work. Our basic aim is to create tricks and get worldwide markets for them,'** says Sam.

FUNTIME INNOVATIONS' ACHIEVEMENTS

The company had an export turnover of over Rs 2.5 crore in 2010–11. Of the 1500 products, roughly 25 percent are custom-made and special-order items. Another 50 percent are items which have been in the public domain for years and which every magician requires. The remaining 25 percent, that is, more than 400 items, are entirely Sam's own creations. No other company in the world sells such a large number of items of its own creation. Sam's business has been a consistent winner of export promotion awards in two categories—the highest exporter of magic goods for the last thirty-five years and the highest exporter of sports goods for the last fifteen years.

Sam's business is in an area which is not perceived as valuable by society. Indian patent laws don't recognize magic tricks, which leads to theft of ideas. Copyright is allowed, but it only partly solves the problem. While the creation of a new product may take years, fifteen days is more than sufficient for it to be copied, if the product is released in India. Hence, the company's main focus is international markets. After a product is released, the company doesn't market it in India immediately. It is instead marketed in countries like the US, Japan, and Singapore. Somebody inevitably copies it and brings it back to India and then sells it at a much cheaper price. But that takes six months. The lifeline of the business is continuous creation of new tricks.

The company has about forty full-time employees. Over 300 contract suppliers are wholly dependent on its orders, besides which there are a considerable number of part-time suppliers. Funtime fails to execute 35 to 40 percent of its orders. It no longer entertains orders from individual magicians and sells its products only to jobbers (big merchants). An organized approach is lacking because in its case demand outstrips supply.

In the early 1970s, Sam also ran an international magic magazine called *Swami* which he later renamed *Mantra*. The magazine brought him considerable fame and he came to be counted among the most creative people in the field of magic. Martin Gardner of *Scientific American* fame, Ed Marlo, the world's greatest card magician, and many other top creative

53

magicians of the world in those times wrote for the magazine. The magic business was growing much too fast for Sam to give time to the magazine, so he stopped publishing it. Now he plans to revive the magazine. In 1997, Kaufman and Company, the world's top publisher of magic books, compiled volumes of *Swami* and *Mantra* into one book, *Swami Mantra*, which sold like hot cakes. Sam has authored numerous other books on magic such as *The Secrets of Magic, Magic with an ESP Deck,* and *Magic with Ease.*

Sam has also been witness to the dramatic shifts that have taken place in the field of magic. '**Today magicians who used to perform in schools, parties, clubs, and puja pandals are in a pathetic condition. On the other hand, event organizers earn handsomely. They are also magicians, but besides magic they organize party games, balloon modelling tricks, etc. So it's a matter of adapting with the times.**'

Age has not taken its toll on Sam. He still feels he has a lot of creative work left to do and a number of books to write. His life tells us about the passion of a real innovator. '**For forty years, my work has been play for me. I work till five in the morning because from 11 pm to 5 am there are no telephone calls, no interruptions, no people talking to me.**'

Sam rues that there is no one capable enough to take over his business, so that he himself can get the opportunity to retire. Magic is a way of life now. Producing new tricks has been the lifeline of his business. His creativity was sparked out of necessity and passion. It is thus difficult for him to find someone who can match his zeal, creativity, and understanding. Sam has been instrumental in ensuring that magic, as a form of entertainment, stays alive. He has dedicated his life to the cause. He has donned the roles of a performing magician, author, and, above all, an entrepreneur in the truest sense.

Sam tells us about an inspiring analogy between an entrepreneur and a bumblebee. '**According to the laws of aerodynamics, a bumblebee cannot fly, as its weight is too large and wingspan too narrow. However, the bumblebee doesn't know the laws of aerodynamics! It just picks up and flies away. This phenomenon is called the bumblebee syndrome. That's the way an entrepreneur should think. There are no rules, you just do it!**'

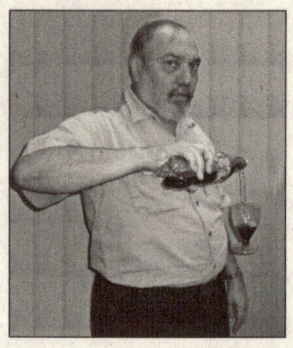

SAM'S SUCCESS TIPS

- You have to love what you do. You have to be involved and dedicated, no matter what. Whatever you do, it has to be twenty-four hours a day. Otherwise you are not enjoying what you do and there is no point in doing that.

- If you have a passion for something, and you are totally devoted to it and know everything about it, you can be a very successful entrepreneur.

THE GURU OF INDIAN IT

Dr Sridhar Mitta

JCB Hall, 1969
e4e Labs Private Limited (Co-founder
and Chairman, Advisory Committee)
NextWealth Entrepreneurs
Private Limited (Founder and
Managing Director)

'Indian IT and I have been fellow travellers' —Dr Mitta.

Dr Sridhar Mitta can be described as one of the heroes of Indian IT folklore but he has always kept a low profile. There hasn't been a historic moment in the IT history of India where Dr Mitta hasn't played a part. He joined Wipro Limited in 1980, becoming their first employee. Since then he has shepherded Wipro, making it synonymous with the success of Indian IT in the global market. During his tenure as Chief Technology Officer (CTO), he helped Wipro become one of the highest valued companies in India. After Wipro, he founded EnThink Inc.—a California based company and co-founded e4e Labs Pvt. Ltd. in 2000 to help budding entrepreneurs to find their feet at the global level. He also founded NextWealth Entrepreneurs Pvt. Ltd. to nurture social entrepreneurship in India.

BORN INTO A BUSINESS FAMILY, Sridhar opted for a career in engineering. He completed his bachelor's in Electronics and Communications from Andhra University in 1967 and came to IIT Kharagpur to pursue his MTech in Electronics and Electrical Communication Engineering. After graduating, Sridhar went to the US to pursue a PhD at Oklahoma State University. He decided in his very first semester at Oklahoma that he would return to India.

But when Dr Mitta finally returned to India in 1973, he found that there were very few employment opportunities for him. He had to choose between a job in a public sector unit, at a government research lab, or teach at institutes such as the IITs. He decided to join Electronics Corporation of India Limited (ECIL) because it was a commercial venture and dealt in development and manufacturing of computers. There, he worked on projects for computer applications in the defence and space sectors.

Dr Mitta kept abreast with the upcoming technologies while at ECIL. The microprocessor was introduced in 1971 by Intel, and Dr Mitta had a keen interest in them. In 1978, he was a member of the team at ECIL which developed the first 8-bit microprocessor-based computer in India, named Micro 78. The Micro 78 systems were sold to the defence and space departments of India for performance of their real-time applications, among others. However, senior management at ECIL did not take the advent of microprocessors seriously. When the 16-bit microprocessor was released, he suggested that they take advantage of the technology. However, ECIL again was not interested.

Around the same time Azim Premji had returned from Stanford University to take the reins at Wipro, then a vanaspati (vegetable oil) producing company based in western India. However, Premji had a grand vision that Wipro would enter high-tech areas like computers. Dr Mitta pounced on the first opportunity and applied for a job at Wipro, joining it in 1980. There were mainly two reasons for joining Wipro: Wipro was interested in microprocessors; and as it was a start-up company, he would have a richer experience for starting his own company in the future. He also felt that there was a huge market potential for computers post IBM's exit in 1977.

Wipro granted money to the Indian Institute of Sciences, Bengaluru, for the development of its first computer and Dr Mitta's responsibility was to deliver it. He worked at the Indian Institute of Science with an MTech student and five professors who were to act as advisers for six months. There was a lot of dilemma regarding the technology Wipro was going to employ for its computer. Dr Mitta remembers having all sorts of discussions regarding the technology, whether to use the 8-bit or 16-bit microprocessor made by Intel or Motorola. They went ahead with the Intel 16-bit microprocessor. And since other hardware parts were difficult to import, they designed, developed, and manufactured the parts themselves.

Wipro fell into a predicament as far as the software was concerned, because building hardware and software at the same time was both time consuming and risky. The only thing close to an operating system available in those days was Control Program for Microprocessors (CP/M), which could be used by only one user and could perform a single task at a time. Dr Mitta started the hunt for a company that made good operating systems. He found a company called Sentinel Computer Corporation in Cincinnati, US. They were designing computers based on the Intel 16-bit microprocessor and had developed an operating system which was multi-user and could multi-task. The company, however, was sceptical about licensing it to Wipro, but Dr Mitta convinced them that they were good guys and followed ethical business practices.

Wipro went to the Department of Electronics, Government of India, to seek permission for the import of the operating system. The department was reluctant as it involved a large amount of foreign exchange it had never dealt with before and prior to Wipro, no other company had approached them regarding import of software. Wipro prevailed upon them by convincing them that the future of the software business in India was very promising and this deal was absolutely necessary for it. However, software wasn't defined in the import–export policy, so the department gave Wipro the licence to import the operating system software under the tag of design and drawings. Wipro had a lot of trouble during the import as well because Customs officials did not understand what the software was about. Moreover, a lot of money was involved, so it made them very anxious. But at the end of it all, Wipro became the first company in India to import software and set the stage for the future of the software industry.

Meanwhile, Wipro was building a strong team for their R&D centre at Bengaluru. It was one of the few Indian companies to place emphasis on R&D rather than on manufacturing and marketing. Back then, it was the norm in IT companies to import complete machines in a deassembled state and then reassemble them. They didn't invest in R&D and manufacturing. It was called 'screwdriver technology'!

Wipro finally launched the Wipro Series 86 range of minicomputers in 1981. The product was excellent; being a microprocessor, it was capable of performing applications usually only possible on mainframe computers. People were astounded to see such high performance from such a small package. The Series 86 laid a strong foundation for Wipro. And the secret behind their success lay in the leadership and expertise of Dr Mitta.

When the UNIX operating system was introduced by AT&T, Wipro approached them for the source code. AT&T refused them because India did not incorporate software protection in its Copyright Act. So, Wipro went back to the Department of Electronics to get the Copyright Act amended to include software in it. In doing so, Wipro became the first company in the world to incorporate Intel 386 microprocessors and UNIX in minicomputers, and this led the Wipro Series 386 systems. Andy Grove, CEO of Intel at that time, sent them compliments for achieving such a feat. Wipro was using its Wipro Series 386 machines to run commercial applications whereas UNIX was only used for scientific applications in the US. They were able to develop many commercial applications with this new series. They even outsourced development of compilers to Softec, a Delhi-based start-up. They were literally practising outsourcing much before the concept existed. Dr Mitta had opened up a whole new platform for Wipro and the IT industry.

Wipro kept on climbing the value chain in sync with Intel's launch of new microprocessors. However, in 1990, when India was going to become an open economy, Wipro reassessed its business model. It realized that bigger companies such as IBM would re-enter India with better resources and technologies, and wipe it out. The only option left would have been to become channels to these international players for their local support. However, it dawned upon Dr Mitta that if the door was open for others to come in, it was also open for them to go out. Wipro decided to take its software skills to the global market since there was a perception that Indians were good at software development.

He met the people at Intel to see whether they could do something for them in the software domain. Knowing UNIX was their forte, Intel agreed to have Wipro's people come over to their set-up in the US to understand their architecture. At that point of time, there was no universally accepted quality process for software development. It was up to Wipro to create the right process that could be acceptable to others. In order to achieve this, Wipro developed a software quality process based on ISO 9000, which was developed for general-purpose factory processes. Wipro was probably the first software company in the world to do so.

Wipro became the pioneer in offshore working; they were building products for the US market from India, while other companies sent engineering graduates abroad after training them here. In 1993, after the famous CBS's *60 Minutes* show depicting Indian engineers taking away US jobs, many large US companies stopped onsite positions for Indians. They started India development centres instead, and then off-shoring burst on to the market scene.

Wipro moved its offerings from UNIX operating systems to network operating systems and branched into hardware and chip design. Year after year it grew at 100 percent and profit margins were in the range of 30 to 40 percent. Most importantly, its customers were happy, as it did things at one-third of the cost.

The reason for Dr Mitta's successes as CTO is majorly due to his commercial outlook. '**I was not an entrepreneur but I was entrepreneurial as I created several businesses within Wipro**,' he says. He was instrumental in setting up the highly successful Interop division for testing projects. This division alone garners a revenue of about $100 million and is the fastest growing division in Wipro.

According to Dr Mitta, there are about a hundred people from Wipro who have started their own companies. This was because Wipro had an environment that allowed its executives to be more entrepreneurial. In 1998, Dr Mitta started EnThink Inc., under the umbrella of Wipro. **'We realized that the ownership of intellectual property developed by us for our customers belonged to them. Hence, we formed a separate products group. The idea was to create our own intellectual property without competing with our customers.'** The group later morphed into EnThink and was incorporated in Silicon Valley. Dr Mitta was the founder and CEO of the company and ran it for about two years.

Dr Mitta was instrumental in the promotion of TiE in India. He has been influential in growing TiE in Bengaluru and making it a great platform for interaction amongst entrepreneurs. In 2004, he became the President of the Bengaluru chapter, which already included illustrious members such as Nandan Nilekani, Kiran Shaw Mazumdar, and Ashok Soota.

Under his presidentship, TiE Bengaluru accumulated surplus funds of Rs 1 crore and bought an office space for TiE. Bengaluru is the only chapter in the world to have its own office.

Dr Mitta's far-sightedness has always helped keep him one step ahead of the others. His latest venture, NextWealth,

DR MITTA AND E4E

In 2000, Dr Mitta co-founded a company named e4e (entrepreneurs for entrepreneurs) along with K.B. Chandrasekhar, his former colleague at Wipro and founder of Exodus Communications. e4e was to be an end-to-end solution for Indian entrepreneurs.

The inspiration behind e4e was a research project of Stanford University named 'Silicon Valley Networks', which sought to explore why Silicon Valley was different and special. The research concluded that when the best brains of the world that are willing to share knowledge with each other assemble together in a small geography, it creates an open ecosystem for learning and prosperity. It also concluded that Silicon Valley could not be replicated. The idea behind e4e was to make Indian entrepreneurs tap into Silicon Valley resources. Today, e4e has over $60 million worth of revenue and 3000 people working for it.

identifies business opportunities with a social intent and helps entrepreneurs to build commercial ventures by providing them with angel funding, mentoring, incubation, etc. One has to differentiate between social entrepreneurship and social activism. It is here that Dr Mitta decided to utilize his corporate experience. The vision of NextWealth is social upliftment through entrepreneurship. The first project that NextWealth undertook was to convert a non-profit blood bank into a self-sustaining, scalable, and financially viable institution.

NextWealth is now busy creating jobs for engineering and other graduates from small towns close to home, with a focus on women and people with disabilities. Graduates from small towns get a good place to work, a decent salary to take home, and a stable career without having to migrate to cities. NextWealth offers its customers 50 percent of the cost compared to cities. Currently, NextWealth has four centres, where about 400 graduates are employed. Each of these centres is managed by a local entrepreneur who is emotionally connected to the location, qualified to manage such centres, and financially capable of raising funds. This can be called the next wave of outsourcing.

Work that was being done in the US and other countries in the past has moved to Bengaluru at less than half the cost. Now, the work being done in that city can be moved to small towns in India at approximately half the cost. NextWealth's target is to create employment for 10,000 people in the coming four to five years and reverse the trend of migration from small towns to cities.

Dr Mitta's career has been an epic journey, and has seen him be a leader of many roles. He started as an IT manager, and then went on to becoming CTO of the IT giant Wipro, to finally founding three successful companies. This has been a true entrepreneurial journey.

DR MITTA'S SUCCESS TIP

- The most important thing that works in favour of Indian innovators is that India is a chaotic country. India provides an ideal environment for entrepreneurship because great ideas are churned out from chaos. There are so many problems which need to be addressed and no one but an entrepreneur can fix these problems.

TECH VISIONARY

Arjun Malhotra

RP Hall, 1970)
HCL (Co-founder)
TechSpan/Headstrong (Co-founder)

Arjun Malhotra is a pioneer of the Indian IT industry. He co-founded HCL, which catapulted the Indian IT sector to the global arena way back in the Licence Raj days of 1975. He was the public face of HCL and was considered the turnaround man for his ability to turn dead projects into extremely successful ones. Much of HCL's initial success was due to Arjun's brilliance in sales and marketing, in addition to his exemplary leadership skills.

ARJUN MALHOTRA SPENT HIS early childhood in Kolkata under the guidance of his maternal grandfather, Dr Sunder Lal Hora, a renowned scientist. In 1954, when his grandfather was the President of the Indian Science Congress, Arjun remembers the great biologist Sir Julian Huxley visiting his home. The family moved to Delhi in 1956 after the death of his grandfather. When Arjun was studying at St Columba's School in Delhi, his father was called for the 1962 Indo-China war by the Indian Army, and his mother, a medical doctor, got a fellowship to go to Harvard University, so he was sent to Doon School, Dehradun.

Arjun joined the Department of Electronics and Electrical Communication Engineering, IIT Kharagpur, in 1965. In the first week itself, he says, '**I realized that there were a lot of people smarter than me.**' Interactions with outstanding professors like G.S. Sanyal and J. Das made a profound impact on his personality. Arjun excelled in academics as well as extracurricular activities and graduated with the prestigious Dr B.C. Roy Gold Medal for all-round performance. He played a number of games—cricket, hockey, football, and basketball—and also participated in dramatics and debates. These extracurricular activities taught him how to motivate friends to focus on meeting goals. He served as the general secretary, sports, of the Students' Gymkhana. The leadership skills he developed during his IIT days came in handy when managing people in his later years.

After graduating in 1970, Arjun's plan was to go abroad to pursue his PhD and fulfil his long cherished dream of joining National Aeronautics and Space Administration (NASA), US. He even got offers from US universities. However, plans do not always work out. He had fallen in love with Kiran, a friend's sister, and decided to marry her. **'I was a little worried that her father wouldn't let her wait for seven years, the time I needed to complete my PhD. I spoke to her father about marriage. And he told me that I had to have a confirmed job before marrying her.'**

Arjun thus joined Delhi Cloth Mills (DCM) as a senior management trainee. DCM was then the fourth largest company in India and paid a handsome salary. His new plan was to stay back in India for a year, get married, and then go abroad. Arjun believes that committing to his lady love at the age of 19 and marrying her at 22 was the 'best decision' of his life.

Meanwhile, DCM, which essentially dealt in fertilizers, textiles, and food products, decided to foray into electronics. Arjun was one of the few electronics engineers in the company and he enjoyed the free hand he got at the company and decided to stay back in India. DCM Data Products, as the new division was called, developed an 8-bit and 16-bit microprocessor-based minicomputer. It was an exciting prospect, and they were convinced that microprocessors were going to change the world.

The strict Licence Raj days, though, were a nightmare for any business. A draconian act called the Monopolies and Restrictive Trade Practices Act restricted the growth of private sector companies, forbidding their entry into new areas. DCM did not want to get into trouble by entering the computer business as it might upset the government. This, however, didn't deter Arjun. Convinced about the power of microprocessors, he and five other friends—Shiv Nadar, Subhash Arora, Ajai Chowdhary, D.S. Puri, and Yogesh Vaidya—left DCM to traverse their own path. They tendered their resignation letters in a single envelope.

Thus, in 1975, they founded Microcomp Limited. Arjun recalls, 'It's funny, when we started we didn't know many other people who had started their own companies in the country.' Starting a company was an 'accident', and purely a spur-of-the-moment decision. He says, 'We thought that if companies like IBM could sell junk in the country, then obviously we could do much better.' Arjun's immediate family was supportive, but his extended family didn't like the idea, calling him crazy for leaving his cushy job and a handsome salary at DCM.

Arjun came from an academic background. No one had ever done business in his family, and the same was the case with the other co-founders too. It was complete bravado. They had the knowledge and they knew the market, but they had no money. In those days, there weren't even any VCs they could approach. Getting a computer manufacturing licence was also a difficult process. A fundraising opportunity came to them in the form of Televista Electronics, a big television manufacturer of the time.

Televista had a plant that manufactured calculators but was unable to sell them successfully. It asked the founder of Microcomp to sell the calculators. Within a short time, they made Televista one of the top selling brands of calculators in India. They put in the money they made into working on their own computers.

The fledgling company tried to cut down on as many expenses in the beginning as it could. They found an office space on Arjun's grandmother's barsati in the leafy lanes of Golf Links, Delhi, and the office chai-pani was taken care of by Arjun's grandmother. Golf Links was one of the upmarket localities and they believed that an address like that on their business cards might give them some credibility. Within a year, the company had expanded into the bedrooms. Very soon, other than the drawing room which served as a waiting area and reception, the office took over the entire house! The company got so big that it finally had to move out of there. Arjun's grandmother was very involved in the company, engaged in making something to eat, meeting people, receiving the guests all through the day.

The next challenge was to get a computer manufacturing licence. The Uttar Pradesh government's UP Electronics

Corporation Ltd. had a licence to manufacture electronics products, but it was not manufacturing computers. UP Electronics was approached by Microcomp, and a joint venture named Hindustan Computers Limited (HCL) was established in August 1976, with its manufacturing facility in a new industrial township near Delhi called Noida. The UP Electronics Corporation held 26 percent stake and the six co-founders pooled in Rs 175,000 from their personal savings and loans from kith and kin.

In March 1978, HCL released its first 8-bit commercial computer in India around the same time as Apple in the US and three years ahead of IBM's PC. However, there was no classification for a microprocessor-based minicomputer or microcomputer for paying excise. The company asked the Department of Electronics (DoE) to put out an official notification so that HCL could pay excise duty and take its computers out of the factory. The DoE said that its microprocessor policy was still not finalized and would take four years. The founders were disheartened by the response. However, after going through the import substitution policy, they found a solution. The company used to import electromechanical machines called accounting and invoicing machines from East Germany. They decided to tell the excise guys, '**Look! We have a keyboard, a display, a printer, so it's basically an accounting and invoicing machine!**' They did this for four years until the policy came out!

In 1980, HCL forayed into international markets by setting up Far East Computers in Singapore. This was a very bold move for an Indian company in those days. The venture was a hit and the revenue was Rs 1,000,000 in the very first year. The company got the software developed in India and provided both software and hardware solutions to clients in Singapore air. Chennai, then called Madras, was chosen as the location for the Software Export Division because the Madras–Singapore air route had short flights and the software could be sent on floppies. The problem was that software was treated as trade and not an industry and was put under the Shops and Establishments Act and not the Companies Act. This meant facing the powerful shop inspectors and a lot of bureaucratic red tape. After numerous consultations with the Tamil Nadu government, software finally got industry status.

Despite the bureaucratic hurdles, HCL had many firsts and emerged as a trendsetter in its field. It was the only company in India to use 5¼ inch floppy drives when 8-inch ones used to be the standard—at that time all the twelve different manufacturers used only the 8-inch floppy drives. Three years later, when 5¼ inch became the standard, all of a sudden HCL was seen as a company which could understand and predict technology. **'In a small company, one wrong decision can kill the company. That's how you play your cards if you really feel that a particular technology can really change the future of the market.'**

Creating India-specific products was the hallmark of HCL. HCL 8C was custom-made for the erratic power conditions in the country. It had a Power Shut Auto Restart (PSAR) unit which ran with a big battery and would hold all the memory and computations of counters exactly where they were when the power went off. The computer would restart exactly from the point where it had stopped, so no data was lost.

For Arjun, HCL was everything. '**It [HCL] was a nasha. After our initial success we started to believe that people do change the world after all.**' HCL recruited the best minds and it was exciting for Arjun to work with them. He had to educate people about things like RAM, ROM, 8-bit and 16-bit processors which we take for granted now. He says that he worked with people three to five years younger than him and they looked to him for answers. However, he didn't have the answers either. It was really exciting as he had to think creatively because every situation was new and uncharted territory.

Running the company professionally was the credo of the founders. They decided that they would take their salaries like everyone else but wouldn't withdraw their stock, no matter how valuable it became. Arjun was the face of HCL and was mainly responsible for the sales and marketing aspects. On its tenth anniversary, the company became the largest computer company in the country.

Arjun still cherishes the 1986–89 period when HCL set up the famed Computer Aided Design and Computer Aided Manufacturing division in collaboration with Apollo Computers. '**These were the years when I used my engineering knowledge to sell solutions.**' In 1989, he took over HCL's failed US operations, and grew them to a phenomenal annual revenue of $100 million, securing HCL's firm entry into the biggest market in the world.

In 1991, on the onset of economic reforms in India, Arjun came back to run the legendary HCL–HP joint venture—the largest joint venture of that time. That deal alone brought in an amount greater than the preceding five years of combined investment in India from the US. In 1996, Arjun set up and ran the joint venture with Deluxe Corporation. He also consolidated and grew the HCL Australasia operations in Hong Kong, Australia, and New Zealand.

HCL has always been a company fuelled by the entrepreneurial zeal of its founders. **'One can probably find more than 150 start-ups and at least thirty to fifty companies in India and overseas where the CEO is an old HCL guy.'**

In 1996, the Internet was just emerging, and Arjun could foresee a lot of opportunities in that field. Since HCL had become a public company, its strategy was to wait and watch, observe the direction the technology would take, and then go after that with full vigour. However, Arjun wanted to be at the cutting edge of technology and play with it as it evolved. He thought that it would not be fair for him to do what he wanted to do with public money.

Thus, Arjun left HCL in March 1998. He thought to himself, **'I must be very lucky. I was 26 years old when the microprocessors came in. I really enjoyed riding that technology "tiger" and witnessed first-hand how it changed the world. Now when I am 49, the Internet has arrived. A**

second major technology paradigm shift is going to happen and I am young enough to have fun in this too!'

Arjun has no regrets about leaving HCL. The one thing he learnt to do very early in life was to not worry about decisions that could not be reversed. He says, **'Worry about the things where the worry can change the outcome of what you worry about, otherwise why worry about it?!'**

In Silicon Valley, Arjun started TechSpan, an IT services and consulting firm, at the end of October 1998, with funding from Goldman Sachs. TechSpan went into the market in early 1999. However, in six weeks he discovered that the market required something else. It was very hot for e-commerce. So TechSpan shelved the original plan, swung the company around, and focused on e-commerce. It clocked a turnover of $67 million in 2000, in just two years of its operation. It was beyond astounding.

When the dotcom crash happened, TechSpan asked its employees to return to its offices in India as the company was not in a position to pay them for sitting idle in the US. Senior people took a voluntary salary cut of 28 percent for three years. One extra person was supported by the entire staff who decided to forgo two days' leave every month till things got better. Technically, the company operated on the assumption that business would improve one day. Never did the company face the prospect of shutting down, though its turnover per year came down heavily from $67 million to $30 million.

In 2003, TechSpan merged with Headstrong; it was the marriage of two different cultures. The plan Arjun had when he started TechSpan was of going higher up the value chain, have a consulting front-end and an outsourcing back-

ARJUN'S ACHIEVEMENTS

Arjun was honoured with the coveted Albert Einstein Technology Medal for the year 2001. He is also one of the founding members of the Society for Promotion of Indian Classical Music and Culture Amongst Youth (SPIC MACAY). He is an adviser to a number of start-ups, both in Silicon Valley and in India, and is currently a member of the Global Board of Trustees of TiE, having previously served as its Chairman.

He is a member of the Executive Council of NASSCOM, a member of the Board of Governors of ISB Hyderabad, and Co-Chair of the PanIIT Alumni Association.

Through a personal endowment, he established the Professor G.S. Sanyal School of Telecommunications, after his beloved professor at IIT Kharagpur, in 1996. He was also among the donors who helped establish the state-of-the-art VLSI chip design laboratory on the campus. In 2001, the golden jubilee year of the institute, he contributed generously to the $5.9 million project to provide high bandwidth Internet access to each student's room. He is also the Chairman of Vision 2020, an alumni initiative to create a $200 million endowment fund for IIT Kharagpur by the year 2020. He was declared a Life Fellow of IIT Kharagpur in 2003.

end. Headstrong had a consulting legacy and TechSpan had expertise in outsourcing. Their merger created a front-end consulting and back-end outsourcing company, something which no one else had at that time.

Headstrong, a global consulting and IT services company with a specialized focus on financial services, had a revenue of $217 million in 2010–11 and over 3700 employees worldwide. The company had operations in seven countries. Arjun served as the CEO till December 2009, and thereafter as its chairman. Headstrong doubled its revenue and quadrupled its profit between 2004 and 2009. Later, in April 2011, Genpact acquired the company for $550 million.

Talking about the entrepreneurial ecosystem in India, Arjun says, 'In our times, you needed the security of a job. My parents told me very clearly that as long as I was studying they would support me, but thereafter I had to take up a job and stand on my own feet. When I look at India's middle class now, I think we have come very far. Now entrepreneurship has become an acceptable norm. People have seen lots of successes and have role models to emulate.'

Since his childhood, Arjun has followed just one simple advice given to him by his parents: 'If you believe in something, then try and do it. Don't do things you don't believe in. Be stubborn.'

And what great advice that is.

ARJUN'S SUCCESS TIPS

- Don't become an entrepreneur because you want to make money. Do it because you have passion and you actually believe in what you want to do.

- Try and recruit people who are smarter than you. If you think that there is no one smarter than you then you are going to get into trouble.

- Don't look at niche market spaces—if the idea doesn't work out then you are left with nowhere to go. Try to take on a bigger marketplace, something like mobile applications today. If you discover that the original idea is not quite good, you can easily switch to another new idea.

STRIKING A CHORD

Dr Kiran Seth

Azad Hall, 1970
SPIC MACAY (Founder)

In an age of iPods, iPhones, and Web 2.0, if a professor at IIT refuses to own a cell phone and drives a Maruti 800, there is clearly something unique about him. Dr Kiran Seth, the founder of Society for Promotion of Indian Classical Music and Culture Amongst Youth, popularly known as SPIC MACAY, has stuck to traditional values and has been leading a lonely crusade for over thirty-four years to save Indian virasat from the curse of oblivion.

SPIC MACAY is a non-profit, voluntary, apolitical, and participatory student movement. It aims to promote awareness among the youth about the classical arts, rituals, mythology, and philosophy that make up the multi-hued cultural tapestry of India. The movement is not restricted to India, and has reached out to many countries across the globe.

THE SPLENDOUR OF Indian classical music has been overshadowed by the razzmatazz of Bollywood and Western pop music, and no one seems to be doing much about it. Kiran emerges before us as a beacon, trying whole heartedly to save our fast decaying cultural heritage and getting young people to appreciate it. With the help of SPIC MACAY, he reminds us that Indian classical music and art forms can help us to reconnect with our souls. 'Catch them young' is his mantra.

Kiran's childhood was spent on the campus of IIT Kharagpur. His father was one of the first professors at the institute. Kiran reminisces, **'I have some lovely memories of the place. It was in the midst of a jungle. I once saw a cobra in my backyard, and later, a tiger. I also distinctly remember an incident when a rogue elephant ran down the road and finally had to be shot down by jawans of the Gurkha Rifles from Salwa.'**

In 1965, he joined IIT Kharagpur as a student to study Mechanical Engineering. **'I learnt a lot of things at IIT which helped make me a better person.'** He stood third in his department and sixth in the institute. He also represented IIT in athletics, basketball, and swimming. He was part of a couple of award winning plays and used to sing Western pop songs. He listened to a lot of Western music, and loved

The Beatles, and found the yearly Green Amateurs Night—a classical music concert—rather boring.

After completing his BTech in 1970, Kiran went to Columbia to pursue his master's and PhD. It was during his PhD that he fell in love with Indian cultural music. In 1972, he happened to see an advertisement in the *Village Voice* regarding a concert by Ustad Aminuddin Dagar and Ustad Fariduddin Dagar. They were presenting a dhrupad recital at the Brooklyn Academy of Music in New York. Kiran and his friends went to check it out, even though they didn't think that the music would interest them greatly. However, by the end of the concert Kiran was walking one inch above the ground. It was the most inspiring event of his life.

Kiran, along with some of his friends, started inviting artistes like Ustad Ali Akbar Khan to perform under the aegis of the India Club of Columbia University. After completing his PhD in 1974, he joined Bell Labs in New Jersey, while he continued delving into various aspects of Indian heritage in his spare time. Meanwhile, Kiran got an offer to teach at IIT Delhi, for which he hadn't even applied. Perhaps it was destiny because by that time his zeal to learn classical music was at a fever pitch. The opportunity of returning to India was too great a temptation, as he had a chance to learn from the master himself, Ustad Aminuddin Dagar.

In 1976, Kiran left Bell Labs and joined IIT Delhi to teach Operations Research, where he continues to teach. He liked the job so much that he stayed on. During his summer vacation, he went to Kolkata to learn music from the ustad himself. He also learnt from Ustads Zahiruddin, Faiyazuddin, Fariduddin, Fahimuddin, and Sayeeduddin Dagar.

In 1977, he formed a group called Mechanical Engineering Final Year Operations Research Group (MEFORG). The group organized its first classical music concert at IIT Delhi in 1978, which turned out to be a complete disaster, with only ten people turning up for it. Kiran didn't lose heart. He says, '**Classical music had touched me deeply. I said to myself, if it can touch me, it can touch others.**' The group was rechristened Mechanical Engineering Final Years (MEFYs) the following year. Their next event was a minor success.

Students took the group to other colleges in Delhi, and then it spread to other cities like Kolkata, Ahmedabad, and Bengaluru. The movement spread organically after that and, from 1979, it came to be known as the Society for Promotion of Indian Classical Music and Culture Amongst Youth (SPIC MACAY). When he started off on the journey of SPIC MACAY, many of his relatives were against this idea. They thought he was squandering away a wonderful research career for some 'stupid gana bajana'. However, his immediate family was very supportive. His parents encouraged him and his father gave him many pointers.

The major problem SPIC MACAY faced in its infancy was getting big artistes to perform for them because of their financial constraints. Kiran shares a particular experience where he tried to persuade the late Ustad Bismillah Khan to perform for them. He was one of the few artistes whom SPIC MACAY had first contacted. 'He [Ustad Bismillah Khan] **was staying at the Crown Hotel in Fatehpuri, Delhi. When we requested him to perform for us, he heard us out and asked how much we would pay him. I said we did not have anything but a small token dakshina to offer. He declined, saying that he had fifty people in his troupe to support, so it was impossible for him to perform for so little. We tried to convince him for the next hour, but to no avail. When we got up to leave, he suddenly had a change of heart and asked us to sit down. I don't know what happened but something we said must have touched him. And he agreed to perform.'**

It was the turning point for SPIC MACAY. With Ustad Bismillah Khan performing for them, SPIC MACAY used his name to persuade other artistes to give performances. Kiran maintains that the artistes' contribution to the cause has been phenomenal.

Another predicament the organization faced in the beginning was the lack of sponsorship. It was a pretty difficult task to get sponsors as SPIC MACAY were little known and seemed to come off as entertainment rather than as a social initiative. **'If we had been educating the underprivileged or dealing with issues regarding women and children, they would have sponsored us. These areas of work are in the tangible domain, while we were focusing on the intangible. The greatness of our country has been, and still lies, in the**

sphere of the intangible, which is much more difficult for the corporate world to comprehend,' he says.

Finally, SPIC MACAY approached the government for funds. The government appreciated their cause and decided to support them in a generous way. Over the years, the Ministry of Culture, the Ministry of Youth Affairs and Sports, and the Ministry of Human Resource Development have continued to support them. Last year, they raised about Rs 10 crore from sponsorships, and a large percentage of that was contributed by the government.

Kiran feels that the lack of exposure has resulted in the lack of interest in Indian classical music and other art forms. He feels it's up to the student community to expand the movement. **'We are doing over 3000 events a year, and it is possible to cover all educational institutions in the country if the youth come forward and take this movement far and wide.'**

According to him, he is not battling the effect of Western music as such. It's more of a clash between popular music and classical music. He thinks that the romance with Western pop music and Bollywood music is fleeting; and that classical music and popular music are incomparable. One is for entertainment and the other for inner upliftment; Michael Jackson entertained, while Pandit Bhimsen Joshi elevated you, yet both are great artistes in their own right. Indian and Western classical music can affect you deeply, provided one is exposed to it repeatedly.

Kiran believes that classical music is not something one can understand and enjoy from the very first moment. The only manner in which classical music reaches the youth of today is through fusion. Kiran believes this is not the solution. **'You can't present fusion music and expect them to listen to classical music. One has to present the real thing again and again, only then can the listener appreciate the depth of classical music and begin to love it.'** In the thirty-three years since SPIC MACAY came to life, it has generated a lot of awareness among the youth regarding classical music. However, he feels that the music has not permeated them. They haven't found the depth as yet, but he believes that they will over time.

The problem, Kiran feels, lies in the fleeting attention span of today's youth. Even though they are brighter, better informed than their predecessors because of the easy accessibility of information through the Internet and television, everything has a format, which needs to be followed in order to derive the maximum benefit out of it. If you are watching television and don't like what's on, you can change to any of the hundred other channels with the simple click of a remote. However, if you want to understand Einstein's Theory of Relativity or read a book by Mahadevi Verma, it requires a lot of patience. Similarly, to appreciate the qualities of Indian classical music, one needs to have patience and faith, both of which are at a premium today. The ability of society to understand things of depth has become that much more difficult. Other than this fact, he feels the response of the youth has been very good.

SPIC MACAY has extended its reach beyond the borders of India. It has expanded to about fifty cities across the world. The organization's promotion abroad is done through a voluntary network of people who know of it or have heard of it. SPIC MACAY has created a separate module for other countries. Kiran strongly feels that Indian culture has a lot to offer to the rest of the world. Just as the Internet and mobile phones are for the whole world, the heritage of India is for the rest of the world to acknowledge. India's biggest contribution to the world can be described in one word—Yog. The biggest contribution of the West has been connecting the people of the world through their mastery in science, technology, business, economics, etc. Connecting with the inner self (through different forms of 'Yog') has been mastered in this country. To live an ideal life, one has to maintain a balance between the connection with the outer world and the connection with one's own soul.

KIRAN AND SPIC MACAY'S ACHIEVEMENTS

Kiran was awarded the much-coveted Padma Shri in 2009 for his selfless contribution to the preservation and promotion of Indian culture and heritage. He won the NDTV Indian of the Year Award in the Arts and Culture category, and received the Distinguished Alumnus Award from IIT Kharagpur in 2009. He also won the Rajiv Gandhi National Sadbhavana Award in 2011. However, he feels that it is not the awards which vindicate his contribution to SPIC MACAY. 'Awards such as the Padma Shri are good things to receive but it's not the ultimate goal. Whatever I have achieved working for SPIC MACAY far exceeds any award I can ever get. The satisfaction achieved is immeasurable.'

SPIC MACAY also organizes cultural programmes in Pakistan as a part of the peace process. Kiran believes that SPIC MACAY can help bridge the divide that exists among the different cultures of the world. 'Our classical music is **a way of connecting with the within. It is a way of life. If you can connect with your inner self, you can connect with anyone. If one is superficial then one is in a state of unrest. On the contrary if one is connected with the inner self, harmony and tranquillity will prevail. Once people begin to feel good internally, there will be fewer conflicts.'**

SPIC MACAY encourages talented young musicians by giving them a chance to perform in its programmes, and has diversified its activities by organizing programmes in folk music, yoga and meditation, crafts, talks, baithaks, and screening of classic movies. According to Kiran, all these are different roads to the same goal. '**If one saw Ganga Devi doing Madhubani paintings, it was a kind of yog she was practising. It depends on the inclination of the individual as to which path he or she chooses to connect with the inner self. The form is incidental.**' SPIC MACAY also emphasizes the need to preserve the fast dying folk traditions, as folk is an essential element of classical tradition.

Kiran hopes that while attending a SPIC MACAY event the audience not only enjoys it but is also inspired by it. It annoys him when people start clapping every 2 minutes in a show. The show should be an inwardly inspiring experience, he feels. Each event ought to be like the one performed by

Ustad Aminuddin Dagar in St Stephen's College many years ago. After he finished his performance, there was complete silence for a minute. And then the audience slowly started applauding. The music had taken the audience to a heightened level of appreciation. This is the power of Indian classical music and our great heritage.

Kiran sometimes still feels they are fighting a losing battle. **'The feeling changes from day to day, sometimes you feel depressed, contrarily you also feel satisfied when you see a glow even in one young person's eyes. The electronic media has captured the mind of the youth. They are constantly connected with the outward world through the Internet and the mobile phone. One cannot be connected to the outer and inner world at the same time.'** It is for the same reason that he refuses to own a cell phone. Kiran hardly ever watches television or goes on the Internet. Even though he feels that the youth wastes a lot of time on the Internet, he feels hopeful whenever he comes across someone trying to find out more about Indian heritage.

While there have been many people who have come and gone, there have been others who have helped SPIC MACAY tremendously and were instrumental in laying its foundation. For example, Babi Barua, a student of Hindu College, Mahendra Malu, a batchmate at Columbia University, and Arjun Malhotra, his batchmate at IIT Kharagpur, backed the organization with money and other support.

Arjun Malhotra quietly advertised SPIC MACAY events

in the Delhi newspapers. The advertisement ran a line at the bottom—Ad courtesy Hindustan Computers Limited. This went on for about a year. Meanwhile, HCL had started their operations in Singapore, and for that they had built a software division in Chennai. However, software in the 1980s was not considered an industry but a trade, and HCL needed to change this in order to conduct business in Singapore. Wrangling with bureaucrats and politicians of Tamil Nadu to convert software into an industry was to no avail. One day, Shiv Nadar (co-founder and current Chairman of HCL) walked up to Arjun and asked him about SPIC MACAY. Arjun wondered why Shiv had suddenly come up with that query. Shiv informed him that some of the Tamil Nadu politicians had come to Delhi and seen SPIC MACAY's advertisement in papers. On seeing that HCL advertised for them, they concluded that HCL was a company with a soul and that they should hear them out. A few months later, HCL was given clearance and software was classified as an industry.

Kiran is an educationist in the truest sense. An educationist looks at the overall development of the young person, and nurtures both the internal and external aspects of students. Without striking a chord or playing a note, he touches the soul of others around him.

KIRAN'S SUCCESS TIPS

- If you want to do something pathbreaking, you need to be inspired first. You have to be passionate about it in a very fundamental way.

- You can't give up; you have to go through the trials and tribulations. People will tell you that what you are doing is foolish but if you're convinced about your idea, no one can affect your decision.

- You might sometimes question yourself whether what you are doing is right or not; in times like these, your resolve will get you through the dilemma.

- Finally, you have to make sacrifices as there is no such thing as a free lunch.

THE THINK TANK

Dr Prabhakant Sinha

Patel Hall, 1970
ZS Associates
(Co-founder and Co-chairman)

Prabhakant Sinha represents the unique breed of people who convert their research activities into successful entrepreneurial ventures. A multifaceted person, he encompasses the roles of entrepreneur, teacher, author, and philanthropist.

His company, ZS Associates, is one of the world's largest sales and marketing consulting firms. The company, headquartered in Evanston, USA, operates from twenty offices across the world and employs more than 1700 professionals. It has serviced over 700 clients in seventy countries. It was named the seventh best consulting company to work for by *Consulting Magazine* in 2009. ZS was also placed second in the 2011 Vault Rankings for Pharmaceutical and Health Care Consulting.

IN HIS CHILDHOOD, Prabhakant Sinha had often relied on kerosene lanterns when he spent time in his village of Jogapur in north Bihar. Today, however, he has been instrumental in bringing an idea of a former employee of his company, Anish Thakkar, and two of Anish's colleagues, Patrick Walsh and Mayank Sekhsaria, to fruition. The idea, a solar lamp, costing just Rs 850 a piece, is changing the face of rural India by replacing dirty and expensive kerosene lamps. Now, Prabha has invested over $700,000 in the company Greenlight Planet.

Prabha's father was a lawyer in a civil court in Chhapra, Bihar. As with any typical middle class family, his family, too, spent money on very few things. The most important of these was education, and Prabha was sent to St Xavier's in Patna, an English-medium boarding school.

Prabha went to IIT Kharagpur in 1965 to pursue Mechanical Engineering. At IIT, he received the merit scholarship most of the time, but says that everyone was super smart. He served as the President of Patel Hall and the editor of *Alankar*, the student newspaper. He played hockey and basketball for his hall. 'The socialization aspects were most important for me. I was constantly learning from others and being exposed to new ideas.'

He graduated in 1970 and completed his PhD in Industrial Engineering and Operations Research in 1974 from the University of Massachusetts, US. His undergraduate thesis at IIT, under Professor K.C. Sahu, was also in Industrial Engineering.

In 1974, Prabha started teaching at the College of Business Administration, University of Massachusetts. By 1977, he had moved on to the University of Georgia. However, he could not resist the temptation of starting a company. '**The entrepreneurial environment in the US infects you**,' says Prabha. His entrepreneurial innings started in 1978 with Comcater. The company set up computer systems for large food service operations and also helped the customers in meal planning. Meal planning involves optimizing nutritional elements for a given amount of money to be spent on food. At that time, computers were still large and bulky and were mostly used in companies for finance and accounting. Minicomputers were just beginning to find a home, in addition to the mainframes. In the state of New Jersey, the company set up computer systems for thirty to forty institutions, including senior citizens' homes and prisons.

The company turned out to be a failure. Prabha learnt two important lessons—lessons about people and focus. First, the success of a company is mostly dependent on hiring talented people. The strength of a team is not just based on its technical know-how but extends to marketing and sales capabilities. Second, one can't do two things—teaching and running a company—at the same time. One can run a business only by fully immersing oneself in it. Prabha's idea was that he would continue teaching and Comcater would be managed by hired people. In this, he was inspired by a company, named Management Decision Systems, run by professors from MIT.

Prabha's next venture, ZS, however, was definitely a winner. The sales force is a very important part of a company. 'Sales force' means persons responsible for selling products or services via direct contact with customers. Members of the sales force are assigned a 'sales territory'. Territories may be defined in terms of geography or accounts. In large sales forces with thousands of salespeople and tens or hundreds of thousands of accounts, the problem of assigning accounts to salespeople is complex. In a dynamic environment with customer and product changes, this problem has to be addressed frequently. That is called sales territory alignment. Addressing this problem was to be the seminal idea that launched ZS. This time, a key partnership was behind much of the success.

In 1973, Andris Zoltners, Prabha's partner-to-be, completed his PhD at Carnegie Mellon University. His thesis on Integer Programming was related to sales territory alignment problems. He subsequently took up a teaching position at the University of Massachusetts. **'We got to know each other while I, as a PhD student, was exploring the use of advanced mathematics in meal planning for the military.**

We co-authored a paper which was highly applicable to the problems of sales force sizing and resource allocation.'

Andris had a friend named Osama, who worked for a company in Indianapolis. Osama's company was facing sales force resource allocation challenges. So he invited both Andris and Prabha to come up with a solution. They figured out that the problem could be solved mathematically, so they set up a computer system to do that. Prabha was at Comcater at that time and also teaching at Rutgers University. **'We engaged ourselves with a number of companies, gaining practical experience by applying our modelling techniques to real-life sales force problems. In many ways, I was even less focused than before.'**

In 1982, Andris presented his and Prabha's mathematical models, addressing their problems to the Pharmaceutical Management Science Association (PMSA). Executives from many of the attending companies were stunned by the model's ability to quickly solve sales force sizing, sales resource allocation, and territory alignment problems. They, for the first time, could see solutions visually in real time on an early Apple computer, with one of them, David Levy, exclaiming, **'I've been waiting my whole life for this!'** Three companies showed interest in applying the models. For the two professors, it was a perfect start.

After helping eight companies, they concluded that there was an opportunity to help many clients address critical sales force effectiveness issues. In September 1983, ZS Group, Inc.

was born, 'Z' coming from Zoltners and 'S' from Sinha. It was soon renamed ZS Associates, Inc. By 1983, they were both teaching at Northwestern University's Kellogg School of Management by day and working on client projects at night.

ZS had an academic birth. The founders applied their research work to real-life problems to help companies, while building a profitable business. Their work was initially supplemented by PhD scholars, but by 1984, they had hired their first MBA graduate from Kellogg.

The year 1985 saw the ZS staff strength increase to more than two dozen, and the university's computer centre was unable to meet the needs of the burgeoning consulting firm. Prabha and Andris, realizing the need and opportunity to expand, collateralized an IBM 3481 mainframe computer purchase with their homes. That same year, the firm released the second version of its automated territory design software.

By 1986, ZS had helped eight of the world's ten largest pharmaceutical companies size their sales forces in the US and Canada as well as in Europe. The firm had already worked on nearly a hundred projects in a dozen countries. The focus on the pharmaceutical industry has remained till date. Even now, close to 75 percent of the company's clients are from this industry. 'There was lot of innovation taking place in the pharmaceutical industry at that time. The industry was expanding very rapidly and our solutions were very good for them. We had no competitors then as our product was differentiated. We were both pioneers and leaders in the space.'

By 1987, it became clear that Prabha could do only one thing, teaching or running the company. The Comcater lesson of focus was more than just a memory. He left teaching to focus on the company full time, while Andris continued his teaching career, retiring only in 2010.

In the early days, ZS had a tough time recruiting and retaining the best talent. Prabha feels this was because of two reasons. First, people's needs go beyond satisfaction from work and salary. The solution was to treat the employees nicely. Second, the company was hiring undergraduates and MBAs at the same time for different jobs. The MBAs were treated slightly better, and this led to well-performing undergraduates leaving the company as they felt frustrated with the double standard. A female undergraduate called Kathy had left ZS because of this issue. She then went on to become the CEO of a huge company. ZS came to refer to this outflow of talent as the 'Kathy problem', and used this as a case study to better the company's staff management.

ZS has helped clients launch hundreds of products through a solid understanding of the key drivers and barriers for successful launches. For this, a huge amount of data relating to the needs and preferences of customers needs to be analysed. In 1990, a ZS partner, Rob Sederman, came up to Prabha saying that he was bored with sales and wanted to go into marketing. He had an idea to track evolving customer attitudes at the time of new product introductions—customers are responsive to marketing campaigns and companies should adopt suitable strategies. '**Now the marketing area is a third of our total business. With responsibility, people innovate a lot.**'

ZS values its association with its clients immensely. Its first client from the PMSA meeting almost thirty years ago still works with them today, and a major chunk of its business comes from repeat clients.

The dynamics of consulting, though, are quite different from the dynamics of a product sale. Prabha recounts an early mistake of ZS. '**What to do when you think the answer is X, but the team leader on the customer side thinks the answer is Y? In our early days we faced such a situation. On one occasion I didn't hold my ground and went along with Y. That company became very unhappy with us as Y gave poor results. They regretted their decision to hire us and didn't work with us for the next fourteen years! We finally brought them back but they never forgave us.**'

The academician in Prabha is still active. He teaches executives at the Kellogg School of Management and Indian School of Business, Hyderabad, and has previously taught at London Business School and Management Center Europe, Brussels, Belgium. He has co-authored several books with Andris. His first book, *The Fat Firm,* was published in 1997 and was translated in several languages and became a bestseller in China. His other books include *Building a Winning Sales*

Force, The Complete Guide to Sales Force Incentive Compensation, Sales Force Design for Strategic Advantage, and *The Complete Guide to Accelerating Sales Force Performance.*

PRABHA'S ACHIEVEMENTS

Prabha is a trustee of the Art Institute of Chicago and a patron of the Telluride Film Festival and the Chicago Humanities Festival.

Prabha was inducted into the Chicago Entrepreneurship Hall of Fame in 2005. He was honoured with the coveted Distinguished Alumnus Award by IIT Kharagpur in 2010.

After living the life of an entrepreneur, teacher, and author, Prabha has embarked on a mission of giving back to society. In January 2010, he donated $2 million towards setting up the P.K. Sinha Center for BioEnergy at his alma mater, IIT Kharagpur. A visionary passionate about protecting the environment, he has decided to bring about a change in policy and attitude towards renewable and sustainable energy through this centre. '**The Center will provide a unique opportunity to apply an integrated and collaborative approach to solve the energy crisis, climate change, and economic challenges in one go. Besides reducing the carbon footprint, bioenergy will help in enhancing the income of villagers and rural communities.**' He has also funded annual scholarships at the University of Massachusetts for women in engineering.

Prabha, a follower of Swami Vivekananda, is the first Asian American trustee of the Art Institute of Chicago where, in 1893, Swami Vivekananda, while attending the World Parliament of Religions, gave his historic inspirational speech—'Sisters and Brothers of America!' Prabha is also a patron of the Telluride Film Festival, and earnestly supports Indian filmmakers. His other loves include photography and travelling to exotic places around the world.

Prabha owes special thanks to his wife Anita and their two daughters for their support in his endeavours. He met Anita at the University of Massachusetts while she was pursuing her PhD in Sociology. Anita serves on the board of the Chicago Foundation for Women.

Looking back at his entire journey, Prabha feels that one has to keep growing to keep going. He moved from mechanical engineering to industrial engineering and operations research, then to applying operations research to sales and marketing issues, and on to broader and more qualitative challenges in sales. Each step was connected to the previous step, although they look illogical, if one compares one step with ten steps ahead, like mechanical engineering with sales. His entrepreneurial idea was just such a one-step-ahead idea. He believes that once you have achieved success, whether through hard work or luck, and you take the lessons from mistakes seriously, it increases the probability of your next success. It's about moving forward with each success and with each setback.

Since 2010, Prabha has been working with David Vinca, a ZS alumnus, who founded eSpark, a company dedicated to making learning fun and effective for primary school children by leveraging the latest tablet computer technology and customizing lessons for each child. Prabha thinks that it will transform the underperforming schools in the US, and his dream is that it will come to the underserved parts of India as well. And next year? **'I am sure I will be on to new learnings, new challenges, and new experiences. Is it not wonderful that there is no end to learning and growing?'**

Academicians have always preferred to stay away from the hurly-burly of the business world. Prabha is definitely a harbinger of times ahead when more and more research activities will be converted into successful ventures to solve real life challenges, and more people he hopes will bring light to the rural masses through solar lamps and education.

PRABHA'S SUCCESS TIPS

- Entrepreneurs can't start just with their ideas. You have to understand your products, customers, and markets.

- You have to immerse yourself completely into the venture you start. It's really difficult to run a venture while you are doing another job.

- Learning from your mistakes is of utmost importance. You cannot figure out a formula and launch your product. You have to figure out the mistakes and make course corrections.

- If you have some success, whether it's because you were smart, or because you were lucky, you have to use the fruits of the success to improve and get to the next level.

MISSION CRITICAL DESIGNER

Ranbir Singh Gupta

Nehru Hall, 1970
Sigma7 Design Group
(Founder and Chairman)

While studying under the shade of trees in his village
school, Ranbir Singh Gupta would take time out to draw
scientific diagrams on the ground or on sand. He still
draws diagrams, but now as a top-notch architect based in
the US. His company, Sigma7 Design Group, specializes
in strategic planning, design and project management
of mission critical facilities for global financial services,
pharmaceutical, and technology clients.

RON (RANBIR) SINGH GUPTA, an Indian American, was given an honorary award in the year 2008 by the Indian ambassador to the US, Ronen Sen, on behalf of the Indian government, for exemplary contribution to community service. This was a proud moment for the son of a family with virtually no educational background.

Ron grew up in Chulkana, a sleepy village near Samalkha town in Haryana. His father had always struggled in business, trying his luck across Kolkata, Assam, and Delhi. To make matters worse, Ron's father contracted Buerger's disease, as a result of which he went through several surgeries, including amputation of one of his legs below the knee. Ron was raised by his grandfather who instilled good work habits in him, like waking up at 4 am and working hard. He went to Chulkana Government Middle School. There weren't enough rooms in the school, so they'd often end up having classes under the shade of trees. Electricity came to the village only when he was in Class 7. Even today, the village does not have running water.

One day, Ron came across an advertisement regarding the IIT entrance exam in an Urdu daily. He was unaware about IITs and without much thought he sat for the exam. Despite not doing exceptionally well at the test, he got into

IIT Kharagpur in 1965. 'Due to my low rank, I didn't have much of a choice and ended up in the Department of Architecture.' Ron laughs loudly, saying he had no idea where Kharagpur was.

At IIT Kharagpur, Ron found his toughest challenge in mastering the English language. However, when he graduated in 1970, he not only topped his department but came second in the institute. After graduation, Ron worked in Vadodara, Gujarat, for seven months. Eventually, he got into the prestigious Carnegie Mellon University, US, for his master's. At Carnegie, Ron also worked full time at an architectural firm to meet his expenses as the scholarship he received covered only the tuition fee.

He graduated in 1973 as a Herbert J. Heinz Graduate Fellow, after which he joined Connell Metcalf, a firm in Miami, Florida. He gradually moved up the company ladder from designer to planner to senior planner, and, finally, to project manager. The job gave him hands-on experience in all the aspects of the design and construction business. At the same time, he taught computer-aided design and architectural design at the University of Miami, Florida.

In 1982, Ron decided to jump into the field of entrepreneurship and founded Gupta Associates in Miami. The US economy was going through a bad phase, but that did not deter him from starting out on his own. He remembers the vow he had taken before leaving India for the US, 'As soon as I get an opportunity, I will start my own company.' His wife, Chitra, managed the finances of the new architectural company. As Gupta Associates worked in an area which did not require much capital, Ron used his personal savings to kick-start the venture. The company got a lot of work orders from the US government.

In its initial phase, a company has to face three main challenges. The first of these is to get work from clients. This requires good marketing skills and an impeccable integrity. Second, to do quality work. Then the clients will come back with more and more work. And finally, to manage the finances well.

Ron emphasizes that hard work was the essence of the success of his company. In the first year, the company approached hundred clients, but got to work with just two of them. In the second year it approached twenty and got ten. After a few years, it managed to work with almost every client that it approached. He says, '**That's the learning process. Don't get disappointed by the failures. You have to be very persistent and only focus on quality marketing.**'

Gupta Associates was acquired in 1991 by Carlson Architecture for a handsome amount, and as part of the deal, Ron could not start a new company for the next five years. He joined the company as Program Director in Pennsylvania. He thoroughly enjoyed the free hand he got as the head of the engineering group of this huge architectural company. Here, Ron mainly worked on energy plants, including nuclear and hydropower plants, and also handled large pharmaceutical and government projects.

Meanwhile, he was appointed a member of the Presidential GSA (General Services Administration, US) Blue-Ribbon security panel, formed pursuant to the bombing of the Alfred P. Murrah federal building in Oklahoma City in 1995. The panel was formed to advise the federal government on design guidelines to mitigate physical threats and vulnerabilities.

In 2000, Ron started his second stint in entrepreneurship. He set up Sigma7 Design Group, specializing in mission-critical facilities, along with five other co-partners, with everyone putting in money from their personal savings. Mission-critical facilities have an ever-growing demand in today's world. These buildings are designed to support and protect the organization's people, equipment, and data to a level that far exceeds standards for normal buildings. A mission critical facility must operate absolutely reliably around the clock, 365 days a year, under any circumstance. It must be able to support the organization's mission despite threats or lack of support from the outside world. Even if electricity or fresh water is no longer available, these facilities must operate using only what is available within. Examples of mission critical facilities include corporate data centres and military installations.

The main data centre of the Bank of New York (now called Bank of New York Mellon) was situated next to the World Trade Center. The data centre housed the computer systems responsible for the financial transactions of this huge company. As the data centre fell along with the twin towers after the 9/11 attack, the bank's financial transactions failed, putting its millions of customers in a quandary. The bank's failure had a cascading effect as the bank was also responsible for facilitating the flow of funds between the Federal Reserve and its member banks. Sigma7 was hired to ensure that such a situation never happens again. **'We were hired to design the data centres in such a way that any incident, whether natural or man-made, including 9/11-type incidents, don't affect the bank's business.'**

Observing the commendable work done by Sigma7 in this particular case, the Federal Reserve Bank of New York, the apex bank of the US, also became a client of the company, asking it to design its data centres.

Among the memorable projects, Ron counts the GlaxoSmithKline enterprise data centre project as one. Located in Pennsylvania, the data centre for one of the largest pharmaceutical companies in the world can withstand even strong hurricanes and tornadoes. The robust steel frame and shell, fabricated from insulated precast concrete panels, ensure this. Its electrical infrastructure systems are designed to ensure no single point of failure, while the mechanical cooling infrastructure is designed for free cooling during the low temperature months. This approach also yields tremendous energy and water savings throughout the year.

RON'S ACHIEVEMENTS

Ron has served as the national chairman of the American Institute of Architects (AIA) Committee on design-build and has received several AIA awards. He has also authored two chapters in the *AIA Handbook for Design-Build Practice*, and has spoken at the 7x24 Exchange, an organisation which holds discussions on mission critical projects.

In late 2007, Ron came across a story about how Alfred Nobel got the idea of setting up the Nobel Prizes. Ron realized that he too needed to do something to leave a legacy behind. Through the Ranbir and Chitra Gupta Foundation, he made an endowment of $1 million in 2008 to set up the Ranbir and Chitra Gupta School of Infrastructure Design and Management at IIT Kharagpur—a first of its kind in India. He was given the coveted Distinguished Alumnus Award by IIT Kharagpur in 2010.

Ron argues that his company is quite different from other architectural companies. First, maintaining a good relationship with clients is taken very seriously, which large companies find very difficult to do. Second, the area in which it works is extremely specialized. Very few companies have this kind of specialized knowledge. Third, the company values talent immensely, so it always tries to retain its core employees. Large companies tend to let people go and instead hire a new person, which may prove disadvantageous for them. Since its inception, Sigma7 has done architectural work for projects whose total construction costs exceed $1 billion. Starting from six people in 2000, this privately held company's staff has increased to nearly thirty-five in 2011. The growth is not only in terms of the number of people or revenue earned but also in net earnings. Sigma7 has become more efficient, which is essential for maintaining high quality.

Ron owes a lot to his wife and two children. Getting unflinching support from family is very essential for an entrepreneur as one has to be away from family quite often. His wife, Chitra, is Vice President in the United Healthcare Corporation, one of the largest insurance companies in the US.

Ron stresses a lot on the need for community service. When people are successful in life, they should do things for the community they live in, whether it's a city or town or village. **'My wife and I have done our best to support the community we live in. We have volunteered for Junior Achievement of America, where we teach high school students on the values of American business and entrepreneurship. We take classes on how to be successful and also help schools in preparing educational programmes.'**

'The world is his who does his job with compassion'— this 2000-year-old quote of the renowned Tamil poet and saint Thiruvalluvar, sums up Ron's life and achievements appropriately.

RON'S SUCCESS TIPS

- If you have an idea, work on it. If you fail, try again. Keep trying. Just stick to it. Don't ever give up.

- Always maintain your ethics and integrity. Never compromise your moral and ethical values.

- Do community service and help others who are not as fortunate as you are.

THE JOURNEYMAN

Bikram Dasgupta

RP Hall, 1973
Pertech Computers Limited (Co-founder)
Globsyn (Founder and Chairman)

Bikram Dasgupta's entrepreneurial journey has been that of a gambler's. From the very beginning, he has made a mockery of conventional wisdom, and has always come out on top.

Bikram was one of the five co-founders of Pertech Computers Limited (PCL), which was at one point the largest PC manufacturer in India. He left PCL in 1995 to start Globsyn, which was single-handedly responsible for the IT industry set up in West Bengal and turning around the industrially deprived state's fortunes.

His book *Minds on Fire—An Infotech Entrepreneur's Journey* is studied at all the leading B-schools in India.

'ORDINARY PEOPLE CAN do extraordinary things' is the doctrine Bikram Dasgupta believes in. It is this belief that helped him scale the colossal obstacles that lay in the way of his entrepreneurial journey.

Bikram joined IIT Kharagpur in 1968. This is where he learnt the essential qualities required to be an entrepreneur. **'The most important thing IIT gave me was confidence, and it helped me in everything I did. If you assemble the best brains and live with them for five years, you feel good, happy, and confident in life.'**

After graduating from IIT in 1973, Bikram joined British Oxygen Company (BOC). There he met one of his first mentors, Mr Balagopalan. **'Your first boss is the most crucial person in your working life. Mr Balagopalan provided me with immense freedom. He allowed me to do things of my own accord, but he also very tactfully restrained me when I went overboard. He has been a great influence on me and I am indebted to him for having shaped my values in life to grow,'** says Bikram.

In 1979, he left BOC to join his hostel senior and college mentor Arjun Malhotra at Hindustan Computers Limited (HCL). HCL was a new company which aimed to kick-start the computer industry in India. Bikram pounced on the opportunity to contribute to this revolution. He was among the core group of professionals who joined HCL in its infancy. His contributions as one of the key market development managers has gone a long way in establishing the market presence that HCL commands today. However, after four and a half years at HCL, the entrepreneurial bug finally bit him.

The year 1984 saw the birth of PCs. The focus was to build a computer which could be used by the common man. The power of the desktop was transferred from a corporation to an individual. It was a major change for society all over the world. For the first time, individuals could do their personal work on a computer. There were a number of software companies, such as Microsoft, that were springing up across the world to cater specifically to PCs. '**In 1984, we, six IIT alumni, founded a company called Pertech Computers Limited to realize our dreams of bringing the PC revolution to India.**' The company was started by Dadan Bhai, A. Mittal, Stephen Aranha, Bharat Goenka, Anil Chopra, and Bikram. Arjun was a soft promoter for the company.

As Promoter Director, Bikram navigated the company through the initial turbulent years. He took a leading role in managing a diverse set of functions ranging from sales and marketing to international business development and new strategic projects. In 1992, Bikram etched his name in Indian IT history when he single-handedly won the single largest export contract worth $50 million, from Dell Computers,

USA. This contract is still rated as the largest single contract in the hardware industry.

Bikram considers this one of the toughest and most rewarding phases of his life. The whole deal was built out of a survival instinct. PCL wasn't doing well and the company was in huge debt. However, they hung in there and tried to see what the possible solutions were to overcome the situation. The only way out was to export as it would bring in foreign exchange. Bikram approached Dell to explore a possibility of business between them. It took him nine months to secure the deal. A deal was forged in which PCL was to sell Dell's PCs in India and Dell bought PCL's motherboards in return. It was a complete win-win deal for both the parties. '**When I returned to India, the prime minister called me to congratulate me on this landmark achievement. It was very satisfying,**' says Bikram. They also set up the largest manufacturing plant to manufacture computer motherboards in India.

By 1993, PCL had become one of the top three PC companies in India, taking Wipro and HCL head on. And by 1994, they were the largest PC company in India, beating HCL. The year 1994 saw PCL come out with its public issue, which was highly successful—the shares were oversubscribed twenty-six times. However, after leading the IPO, Bikram decided not to rest on his laurels but leave PCL to explore other areas.

Bikram feels that in an entrepreneurial venture where five or six people get together, they tend to branch out differently as the years pass by. They start off with a common philosophy, but ten to twelve years down the line, they tend to be different individuals. It takes a totally different kind of leadership to govern, or rather, contain five people, who themselves are entrepreneurs. He feels HCL has done it with relative success and Infosys, exceptionally well. It is, however, not possible most of the time. When people evolve differently over time, they tend to move on in different directions. This is exactly what happened at PCL. After the public issue, Bikram and the others came to the conclusion that each of them should follow their own destiny, and PCL should have one boss.

Bikram had become very famous after his legendary deal with Dell. He was invited to many seminars to talk about his experience during the Dell deal. At one such seminar in Kolkata, named Gateway 95, he says, '**Government officials spoke to me and told me that being a Bengali, I should come to the state and set up the IT industry out here.**' They promised him all possible help. The state government was proactively pushing industry-friendly policies. They were very eager to build the IT industry; all they wanted was a person who could stick his neck out and say, 'Yes, I'll do it!'

Bikram recalls, '**People told me I was crazy to do something out here in this state. However, entrepreneurs are illogical people.**' Most people thought Bikram was a fool to go to Bengal, which had a tainted reputation as far as its work culture was concerned. A number of companies were reluctant to set up their units in Bengal due to the notoriety of the much maligned labour unions and the bandh culture. However, Bikram felt very comfortable there. '**Bengal was a huge opportunity for me. I was passionately driven to think that I could change the way the next generation of youngsters would perceive Bengal and how Bengal would be perceived outside.**' Moreover, he had no competition at all. It allowed him to do things in his own way. He could afford to make mistakes, which perhaps wasn't possible in a place like Bengaluru. Yet he knew that there would be many difficulties when he started.

Bikram foresaw the need for a business model built around the fundamental concept of infrastructure and institution, which Bengal lacked, to serve the knowledge economy. In 1995, he conceptualized Globsyn as a group of companies. The idea was to create institutions where the next generation of professionals from Bengal could be trained, and infrastructure for the IT industry could be developed. And Bengal needed that more than any other state.

Globsyn allowed Bikram to discover a different spectrum of entrepreneurial skills. He had to do things he had never done before in his career. At PCL, Bikram had been known as a hardware person, dealing with PCs, systems, motherboards, etc. With Globsyn, it was totally different: he had to build a whole new ecosystem. It required much more than marketing hardware and software, and he had to build a solid infrastructure and knowledge base to nourish the industry. One of his first ideas was to create state-of-the-art workspaces which would cater to global businesses. Infinity was a product of that vision. Globsyn opened Techno Campus, a software finishing school, where people were trained to efficiently develop and manage acquired software projects. This project resulted in their software business, which gathered momentum after the acquisition of the publicly listed company, Synergy Log-in Systems Ltd., in 2006.

In 2002, Bikram started Globsyn Business School, which aims to deal with people at different levels, be it behavioural, developmental, or spiritual. 'The basic idea behind the business school was to understand first how to make a machine work, and then build an environment where the machine can work. After doing so, you train people to work with the machine. Finally, you deal with people and make them a part of this entire journey. This whole process is what makes the journey.'

Today, Bikram is focused on diversifying his businesses to the next level of people involvement and skills development. Globsyn set up a joint venture with the National Skills Development Corporation called Globsyn Skills and is building a large structure to cater to skill development in twenty-one different sectors, predominantly in the eastern part of India. He has taken life beyond IT and cities by bringing various other sectors like retail, hospitality, manufacturing, construction, automobiles, and healthcare to towns.

When Bikram started Globsyn he once again found a supporter in Arjun Malhotra. Arjun has continued to be a strong influence in Bikram's entrepreneurial journey. 'He has always been there whenever I needed his help and has supported me in whatever I did. He is an investor and a part of the Board of the governing council at Globsyn. He is like family to me. There are few guys who are totally unreserved in their way of living and yet totally respected; Arjun is one of them.'

What's next in Bikram Dasgupta's epic journey? He promptly answers, 'Globsyn is just 13 years old. We have miles to go. However, we are an aspiration model. Our core being is "taking people to the next level". It's a never-ending journey.'

Indeed, and it's an exciting one too.

BIKRAM'S SUCCESS TIPS

- Every entrepreneur comes across some troughs in his route to success. Lows are a part and parcel of life. You just need to hang in there. If you feel strongly about what you do and it makes sense to your consumers, things will turn around.

- There are gaps to fill in our society. Identify those gaps, feel strongly about it, then go ahead and fill them. You will always be in business if you keep filling gaps.

- Finally, aspire. Don't fantasize. Innovation is mostly common sense, which comes to you one second earlier than to others.

THE MASTER BUILDER

Praful M. Kulkarni

RK Hall, 1974
gkkworks (Founder and CEO)

Praful M. Kulkarni's story is that of a village boy who, despite all odds, made it big in life. His company gkkworks provides planning, design, design-build, programme/construction management, and general construction services. gkkworks is ranked as a top construction management firm in the US by Engineering News Record.

The firm is listed among Zweig White's top 100 fastest growing design firms Hall of Fame, having made it to the list for more than four years. The company has more than $200 million in revenue and 300 professionals located in the US and India, with headquarters in California.

PRAFUL DID NOT OWN a pair of shoes until he was 11 years old. And now the buildings designed by his company dot the landscape of many cities around the world. This is no small achievement for Praful, considering he was born and raised in a village near Nashik, Maharashtra. 'I knew I had to study hard to get out of the rural mindset. Otherwise, I would have ended up being a clerk or a farmer or something like that. As far as food was concerned, my family was able to afford that, but clothing definitely was an issue. Looking back, it seems it was a very difficult life, but I was happy growing up the way I did. That's the real world for a lot of folks in India,' he says.

Ultimately, all his hard work paid off and the penurious village boy landed with a coveted seat in the Department of Architecture at IIT Kharagpur in 1969. Praful recalls his first year at the institute as being tough as his was a school where the primary medium of instruction was Marathi, and getting adjusted to English in a short span of time seemed a Herculean challenge. Overcoming this limitation, he graduated from IIT in 1974 with an Institute Silver Medal for topping his department. His projects were the winning entries in a couple of annual conferences of the National Association of Students of Architecture.

In addition to his studies, Praful also actively participated in extracurricular activities. Although being in charge of the lighting and back-drafts required in dramatics sometimes necessitated him to be awake till late in the night, he found the experience fun. The IIT experience was not just about studying but also about taking active leadership roles which were to come in handy in his future entrepreneurial venture.

A scholarship from the prestigious Rockefeller Foundation allowed Praful to pursue a master's degree in architecture from the Illinois Institute of Technology in Chicago, US. The institute's architectural school's founder was the great modern architect Ludwig Mies van der Rohe.

On completion of his master's in 1976, Praful did a year of practical training with Skidmore, Owings and Merrill (SOM), a premier architectural firm, after which he decided to return to India. Unfortunately, he could not find a job. Left with no option, he returned to the US and carried on with his job as an architectural designer for the same firm in Chicago. He worked on the spectacular Hajj terminal in Saudi Arabia, meant to handle millions of pilgrims flying in within a week at the airport for the holy pilgrimage.

The successive years saw Praful move from one job to the other. In 1979, he shifted base to Columbus, Ohio, to work for Karlsberger, a 100-people architectural firm specializing in healthcare design. In 1982, he joined Dalton and Newport, a bigger firm in Cleveland, Ohio, as a healthcare planner. It was a tough time as firms were rapidly closing down, but

Praful tried to make the most of what he got. For instance, he asked for an opportunity to promote the firm's healthcare planning business, an otherwise weak area for the company. This helped him in developing his sales skills.

It was in 1986 that URS Corporation, a giant engineering design firm, acquired Dalton and Newport, and Praful was duly sent to Southern California to start a URS office in the region. He was surprised at the company's decision to entrust him with such a huge responsibility as he was just 33 years old at the time. The branch turned out to be fairly successful, and within three years had over a hundred people on its payroll. Praful gradually rose to the rank of Vice President and Managing Director of the Southern California region.

His never-ending quest for knowledge made Praful pursue an Executive MBA in 1991 from Pepperdine University in Southern California to understand the fundamentals of business. Having been constantly criticized for not possessing adequate management experience, the MBA degree ensured that he was competent enough in that area as well, transforming him into a complete businessperson.

The vision for gkkworks was formulated in his MBA thesis where he postulated that when companies got very large, management silos emerged. This was the case with URS, a very large publicly listed company. In the professional services industry, they become silos in planning, silos in design, and silos in construction, and typically, silos don't talk to each other. The common practice now in the US is that architects just design buildings followed by construction managers and contractors who build them with little or no collaboration with the architects.

Praful always dreamt of becoming a 'Master Builder' with the vision of integrating all these different entities together and creating an effective alternative. The aim was to set up a company which provided an array of services ranging from planning to design, to construction and construction management, and customizing them to meet the individual needs of prospective customers.

Immediately after the completion of his Executive MBA, Praful's dream was fulfilled with the establishment of gkkworks in Irvine, California, aided by the financial backing of two friends-cum-investors. Construction management businesses do not require a high capital investment and a total of $150,000 borrowed from the two friends plus another $50,000 obtained by mortgaging his own house was sufficient to get the company rolling.

He says, '**Becoming an entrepreneur involves taking risks. When one is young, it is easier to bet on everything, but as one grows older, jumping into entrepreneurship becomes increasingly difficult as one has the burden of other personal responsibilities looming large over one's head.**' Even though Praful started out when he was 38 years old, it was not late. From his experience, an entrepreneur typically starts in his late twenties into the thirties, when the key entrepreneurial skills develop.

When the company started out, it had nothing to show in its portfolio. Their team of three people had a hard time convincing clients of their capabilities. They worked on the 'ratchet effect'. That is, they got work, then they hired more people, made sure they did good work so that money started coming in from the clients, and then they again hired more people and got more work. This way, the business kept growing.

According to Praful, a company in its nascent stage primarily faces three main challenges. First, in order to start the business, you have to get work. Marketing is very important in this regard. Second, you have to produce quality work which can be ensured by getting the right set of people. Third, you must be able to manage the finances—make sure there is enough cash flow. All these skills, namely, marketing, production, and management, need to come together for ensuring a successful start-up.

The turning point for the company was the Los Angeles earthquake of 1994. It created a lot of opportunities for the firm as it got various projects for assessing the damages caused to buildings by the earthquake and retrofitting them. In the late 1990s, the company got a design-build project for a number of schools in the Los Angeles Unified School District. The company hit the bull's eye by winning a project at the Loma Linda University Medical Center, California. The project's total cost was a huge $1billion!

Praful's innovative method of establishing a division devoted to construction management is what distinguishes him from others who follow the same stagnant approach to architecture. It involved overseeing the subcontractors and making sure a construction job got done on time and within budget.

Mixing conceptual and practical aspects is often a source of conflict between architects and builders. There might be someone who can design on paper, but when one goes to build, it may be impractical. It's rare to have a company doing both. At gkkworks, there are designers who can think in abstract and conceptualize design, and then there are people who are experts in construction and construction management. So the drawing of the building or project is followed by precise construction arguments, after which the builders can build. For the company, having everything in-house makes the construction process efficient, as it negates the possibility of the architect blaming the construction crew or vice versa.

The company specializes primarily in constructing three types of buildings, laying specific emphasis on building types that serve the needs of the community: The first specialization is educational buildings from primary to higher education; the second is healthcare and hospitals; and the last is government buildings, which include city halls, civic centres, libraries, fire stations, courthouses, etc. gkkworks provided pre-construction and construction management services for a $300 million project on a new police administration building in the city of Los Angeles.

In the year 2007, gkkworks added another feather to its cap by acquiring the Community College Services Group (CCSG), a company specializing in higher education planning. CCSG helps universities plan for their future by defining demographics and determining facility needs based on the programmes offered. Thereafter, the planning, design, and construction management works follow. The acquisition has provided the opportunity for early interaction with higher education clients.

Praful fondly remembers perhaps the greatest tribute he received. The former President of the US, Bill Clinton, thanked him in 2003 in his speech at the dedication of William Jefferson Clinton Elementary School. Clinton expressed pride in seeing his name affixed to the first elementary school in Compton in thirty-five years. Praful says, '**I got goose bumps. He is a very charismatic man. When he speaks to you, you think he is 100 percent with you.**'

gkkworks has also supported IIT Kharagpur in preparing a master plan for Vision 2020, a project meant to enhance global leadership and excellence in technology, education, research, and innovation in the institute. It is a very sentimental and emotional experience for Praful as it allows him to do something special for his alma mater.

Praful always had the desire to increase the company's footprint in his homeland, India. This was accomplished when in 2002, eleven years after founding gkkworks, the company opened its first office in India. The company is currently engaged in designing a mixed-use commercial high-rise in Mumbai, the Kohinoor Square Tower. Working with its principle of environmental sustainability, the company is using the best suitable practices to ensure that the building gets a 'LEED Gold' certification. LEED is a rating system for green buildings intended to improve performance in metrics such as energy savings, water efficiency, carbon emission reduction, and improved indoor environmental quality. The building, named after the legendary diamond associated with India's history, would have a diamond geometrical design involving triangular shapes layered on to the building's mass and façades, through clearly defined planes and opposites: void and solid, opacity and transparency. The glass-surface building, with features like rainwater harvesting and biowalls, is set to become a global icon symbolizing the future of India.

Traditional buildings consume 40 percent of the total fossil energy in the US and the European Union. What would happen if we had net zero energy use buildings? gkkworks has taken an active leadership role in ensuring this. Pierce College, USA, is a net zero energy use building project. The solar panels installed will meet the building's electricity needs, while the solar water heaters and utilizing natural sunlight with the help of skylights will also lead to zero carbon emissions annually. **'That's where we want to go, that's the overall perspective,'** he says.

PRAFUL'S ACHIEVEMENTS

Praful is a Fellow of the Rockefeller Foundation and serves on numerous boards, including the IIT Foundation, the National Design-Build Institute of America, the Community College Facility Coalition, and Pepperdine University's Graziadio School of Business and Management. He is a member of the American College of Healthcare Executives and the Hospital Association of Southern California. He has also served as Highway Safety Commissioner for Los Angeles County. He is the recipient of the world renowned Ernst & Young Entrepreneur of the Year Award in 2011.

Besides promoting eco-friendly buildings, Praful is also a big promoter of saving paper. If he takes his laptop out of the office, he makes sure that he has everything needed. His email messages have a footer containing a tree in a landscape, with a line written in green saying, 'Please consider the environment before printing this email.' This is born out of his belief that taking care of the community one lives in contributes immensely to being a complete individual.

Praful is grateful to his family for their support of his endeavours and for their encouragement on the numerous risks he took. He believes that having this kind of support from one's family is very important at the start-up phase when one is faced with challenges like lengthy work hours and managing a whole demographics of people.

Praful believes that building is a mature profession that has existed since time immemorial. In such a business, if one has the ability to take a mature entrepreneural approach, there is a better chance of tasting success than a conventional entrepreneur who fails and succeeds.

PRAFUL'S SUCCESS TIPS

- Know what's going to work. Get the required technical skills and then get some experience in the business world.

- Make sure that you keep going back to the three areas: marketing, production, and management. The biggest mistake people make is to excel in just one area like management or production, which is never enough. You need marketing, management, accounting, and finance functions to go along with it. Even if you don't have these skills, make sure your partners do.

THE MARCH OF THE GEEK

Dr Sunil Gaitonde

RK Hall, 1983
GS Lab (Founder and CEO)

Sunil Gaitonde can be described as one of those people who were born to make spectacular breakthroughs in technology. Unlike the stereotypical geek, he puts his trust in people over ideas—a philosophy which he has applied to all his start-ups.

Today, he is a serial technology entrepreneur who has founded three companies, two of which were acquired. The first of these was Internet Junction, which was acquired by Cisco, and the second, Sarvega, was acquired by Intel. He is currently the CEO of Great Software Laboratory, and is on the IIT Foundation board and a charter member of TiE.

WHEN ONE TALKS ABOUT a boy who grew up in the Shivaji Park locality of Mumbai, one immediately thinks of a famous Indian cricket player. Even though Sunil Gaitonde played and grew up among children who went on to play cricket for India, he chose a completely different stage to make his mark.

As a child, Sunil read voraciously and collected as many books as he could get his hands on. He would then lease out his books from his tiny library for some pocket money—the seeds of the successful entrepreneur he was to become later on. However, Sunil's journey to success started rather alarmingly, with a series of electric shocks while playing with circuits. The shocks, however, did nothing to curb his fascination for gadgets and electricity, or his fixation on becoming an engineer. He says, '**I had my fair share of "shock experiments" with electricity. I was a decent student and wanted to be an engineer from very early on. For me, there were never two ways about it.**'

This love for engineering led him to join IIT Kharagpur. Sunil was admitted in the Electrical Engineering Department. All his life he had lived in a homogeneous society where he spoke no other language but Marathi, all his friends were Marathi, and he'd even studied in a Marathi-medium school. His experience at Kharagpur was a complete eye-opener. '**For** the first time in my life I was exposed to English and to people from different societies and cultures. It was perhaps one of the best learning experiences of my life.'

After completing his BTech in 1983, Sunil set off to the US to complete his MS and PhD in Computer Engineering from Iowa State University. After this, he joined IBM in Rochester, Minnesota. However, Sunil could not be held captive to a routine, run-of-the-mill job. He wanted to come out with some new and exciting product. He wanted to satisfy both the geek and entrepreneur in him.

A few years later, Sunil was already juggling with some ideas of his own. He had designed a new kind of mouse, and came to India to try and find someone who was willing to manufacture it, but no one was interested. He tried several other ideas later, but again there was no interest for them. In 1993, Sunil went to San Francisco and, together with Krish Ramakrishnan, Ratinder Ahuja, and Manoj Goel, started a company, Internet Junction.

They came across a tool called the Mosaic Browser, an Internet browser for UNIX, which was an alien technology at that point of time. They thought it was pretty cool. 'We were geeks; we thought if we needed a browser, probably everyone else did. So we decided to build it for Windows,' says Sunil. However, their plans were late. While Netscape, which had more money and was more adept at building this technology, was founded a bit later, it went on to revolutionize the World Wide Web industry, by building the first web browser which could be used on any operating system. They also had James Clarke on board, who had already co-founded Silicon Graphics, which was a huge success.

Sunil and his partners changed their focus to 'ipx to ip' gateways. They were working on a technology which gave users an easy way to connect to the Internet without having to install a lot of other software and using resources on many computers. It was tough going. They were unable to raise money for the company. They had full-time jobs during the day and worked on their products by night. Sunil was working 18 hours a day to keep up.

The hard work eventually paid off in the form of a lucky break. Cisco, a company which was looking to venture into PC-based products, acquired Internet Junction. Cisco was like Google and Facebook of the early 1990s. There was a joke in Silicon Valley at that time—that you either worked for Cisco or were going to work for Cisco. Sunil and his team were finally in the big game.

At Cisco, Sunil always felt at home. The entire team of Internet Junction had shifted to Cisco, and they were given complete freedom to create their own products.

Sunil had moved to Chicago in 1998, but he had to travel every week to San Francisco. He used to hate this routine. A chance meeting with John Chirapurath and Girish Juneja, both from the University of Chicago, at a TiE event led Sunil to bigger things. They had an idea, which he helped them evolve. Even though the particular idea didn't pan out, Sunil liked working with John and Girish.

In 2000, Sunil left Cisco and started Sarvega with John and Girish. They built an appliance that processed XML (XML appliance) and created their company around this product. Raising venture capital in those days was a tough job because of the Internet bubble burst, which made investors sceptical of companies dealing in Internet technologies. However, this did not affect Sunil or his team's morale; they had firm belief in themselves. They were able to raise $25 million for the company. Sunil recalls, '**It was a painful experience. We raised the first round of funding five days after September 11. We had a great team and a really good business plan. There were a lot of uncertainties, but the investors were impressed enough to give us money.**'

SUNIL'S TAKE ON VENTURE CAPITALISTS

'There is a rule in sales that once you close a deal, you don't try to continue selling. For example, while raising funds for Sarvega in 2001, I had convinced a VC to invest in us. As he was going to sign the deal, I made an additional presentation that wasn't required. Something went wrong and he backed out of the deal. Since then I have not forgotten that rule.

'It's not the idea which matters but the execution which brings you success. I reiterate what I learned from a VC, "Ideas are a dime a dozen!" Remember, there isn't a single idea which no one else has thought of before. An idea will not stay unique for long, so it is important to focus on the team, differentiation, and execution.'

Sarvega was acquired by Intel in 2005. Sunil doesn't regret selling the company he had built with his own hands. He says, '**At the end of the day you are a businessman. When the chance came to sell the company for a good price, we took it.**' After selling Sarvega, Sunil got together with his childhood friend Shridhar Shukla, former COO at Persistent Systems, to start GS Lab in Pune, India. They saw that India lacked companies that had their own intellectual property and decided that this was a good opportunity to create their own company.

Sunil feels that places like Google, Amazon, etc., are able to build world class products because they have access to a highly experienced technical pool. '**The average experience of the technical team at Sarvega was over fifteen years. In India, it is difficult to find people with even ten to fifteen years of technical experience. By the time they reach the age of 35, they digress into management, whether or not they are good at it,**' he rues.

However, he can see that the situation is changing and there are increasing opportunities for building high-tech start-ups in India, especially in fields where the country heavily depends on imports. Also, there are a lot of VCs who are coming to India, and many exit options for start-ups are becoming available. The lack of an experienced technical pool will definitely rectify itself in coming years, he feels.

The core aim at GS Lab is to create new, cutting-edge technology products. Sunil wanted to build GS Lab in a bootstrap fashion. He did not want to spend his time on raising funds for the company, and wanted it to be financially self-sufficient. There are two divisions in the company, one which builds products for other companies, wherever they have expertise; and the other, a smaller division, concentrates on intellectual property building. They try and solve the routine problems in the bigger division in a scalable way. If there is no customer interest in the product made by the bigger division, they consider it as a regular IT project and move on. Currently, GS Lab is spinning out a product called 'K-Point', which is a flexible platform for online teaching and training.

Geeks fall in love with their ideas and sometimes this can be harmful for a technology company. Sunil feels most technology companies pick up a complex technology problem and come up with solutions, and then see if there is a business plan worth their bucks there. He did the same for his first two companies. He thinks that technology companies should review whether their approach towards the problem is correct, if the solution they are proposing is right, and if the business model is going to work. Sunil now advocates a customer validation approach. **'You have to talk to tens of thousands of customers. It is the customer who needs to approve the idea first. You should be in constant touch with your customers. Till the point they start paying you for solving their problems.'** Quoting from Steven Blank's *The Four Steps to Epiphany*, he says, **'Opinions are in the building, facts are outside!'**

After starting modestly with just three employees, GS Lab now has three facilities with 140 plus employees. Each of GS Lab's three facilities is under a multi-year lease.

Sunil has always made it a point to work with people he has fun working with. He likes people with high integrity and energy. He believes that attitude is one of the most important things to look for when choosing a partner to form a start-up with.

Sunil is on the boards of many start-ups, and GS Lab itself has worked with more than forty start-ups in the last seven years.

With the entrepreneurial landscape fast changing in India, particularly with respect to technology start-ups, Sunil's pragmatic approach is worth emulating. His entrepreneurial journey is a perfect lesson for the geeks who seek to become millionaires, while pursuing their passion for technology.

SUNIL'S SUCCESS TIPS

- Be good in the domain in which you want to build a product.

- Understand what your customers want and accordingly implement your business idea.

- Start young—you will get more time to make mistakes and rectify them. As one gets older it gets harder and harder to sustain a mistake.

PERSISTENCE PAYS

Dr Anand Deshpande

Patel Hall, 1984
Persistent Systems
(Founder and Chairman)

Way back in 1990, when contemporary software companies opted to provide only services to rake in the moolah, Anand Deshpande dared to believe that software product development could not only be done from India, but would be the future of the Indian software industry. He made software product outsourcing an integral part of the business model for his company, Persistent Systems. It was a conviction that was amply justified in the years to come.

Headquartered in Pune, Persistent has a presence across three continents, with nine development centres in Europe, North America, and Asia. The company—a leader in outsourced software product development services—registered a revenue of over $170 million in 2010–11. It also won the NASSCOM Innovations Award in 2008.

YEAR 1990: DR ANAND DESHPANDE was working at Hewlett-Packard (HP) Laboratories in Palo Alto, California. He was pursuing his dream job in the same building as the legendary founders Bill Hewlett and Dave Packard. Life was as plush and comfortable as it could get.

However, Anand was going through a phase of indecision. He had to decide whether to continue with his cushy job or return to India—his motherland. For starters, his family wanted him back in India. To add to that, Anand had an exciting dream of starting a company in India. This is how Persistent Systems came into existence in May 1990.

Anand grew up in Bhopal, where his father was employed in Bharat Heavy Electricals Limited (BHEL). In 1979, he went to IIT Kharagpur. He was in the third batch of the Department of Computer Science and Engineering at the institute. Besides being good at academics, he represented the institute in swimming. The department batch was quite small, with just eighteen people. 'I found out that we were competing against one another when we used to apply to universities for available opportunities. I talked to them and convinced them that by cooperation we can have a better success rate, not by being secretive. Let people declare beforehand where they intend to apply, so that not many apply there. Even if more than one applied to the same university, we made sure that they got recommendation letters from different professors.'

Anand's department batch was exceptional. Rajiv Gupta went on to found Confluent Software (now owned by Oracle Corporation) and Securent (now owned by Cisco). Subodh Gupta became a social entrepreneur and runs Safal Solutions, which develops customized IT solutions for NGOs and promotes microfinance, health, education, and livelihood. After passing out from IIT in 1984, Anand moved to the US to pursue his PhD in Computer Science from Indiana University, Bloomington. He joined HP after earning his doctorate in 1989.

When Anand decided to quit HP and start Persistent, it was with an aim to build a software called query optimizer for database systems. 'As a small company, one must identify a niche market and seek to be the best in that niche,' says Anand.

At a time when software product companies were hardly visible in India and software services companies were hogging the limelight, Anand dared to break the pattern. He explains the difference in approach to a product and services company. 'The way a services company works is that you have an IT project, you have well defined requirements, and then you have trade-offs between time and management. On the other hand, when you do product development, the first thing that you have to decide is the launch date for the product. The next thing is to decide on the budget—that puts a cap on how many people you can engage. You start building the product in a way that you can get the best possible product within the time and money framework. It is quite challenging as you decide the time frame without knowing what you are trying to build.'

It is said that getting the first customer is the most difficult task for a new company, but in Persistent's case, it was a bit unconventional. Its first customer was a French company called O2 Technologies, which built object databases. Anand had known the founder of O2, François Bancilhon, professionally. When Anand was working at HP, François was on a short sabbatical there, and sometimes both of them used to commute home from work together. 'When I told him that I was planning to go back to India and would like O2 to be my customer, he laughed. He commented that he knew many Indians who talked about going back to India but none of them ever did. So, in the first place, he did not believe that I would go back. However, on the off chance that I did go back, he promised to give me work.'

The next customer was Data Parallel Systems, Inc. (DPSI). It was a company formed by Tim Bridges, Anand's colleague at Indiana University. While they were both graduate students, they had applied for a grant which formed the basis of DPSI. Anand has always believed that trust should be the core foundation of any enterprise. Getting the first two customers testifies to his belief.

152

India's rise as an IT powerhouse has been credited to a considerable extent to the establishment of software technology parks (STPs), an initiative of the Government of India. STPs provide physical infrastructure and tax incentives. The Pune STP was the first such park to be established in India, in March 1990, by the Department of Electronics (DoE). The space was allocated to thirteen companies.

Persistent Systems was not a registered company at that time and hence wasn't allotted any space. The company was registered in May 1990. **'While we were promised that we would get space in the STP as soon as we got registered, nothing really moved. None of the companies that were allotted space in the STP started operations and no additional space was acquired,'** says Anand. While Persistent already had work orders from its two clients—O2 and DPSI—to execute, the company was forced to wait to get space. It was frustrating for a young man who had just quit an excellent job in the US and returned to his motherland with a lot of hope. Anand quips, **'I must say I used at least some of my time well. I got married soon after I got back from the US.'**

As a final attempt to get space allocated, Anand posted a letter to N. Vittal, the then Secretary of the DoE on March 11, 1991, which was a Monday. On Tuesday evening, the senior director at DoE requested him for details. In the meantime, Vittal invited the director of STP, Pune, to Delhi and in Thursday's meeting, asked him to vacate his own office in the STP. The director of STP, Pune, called Anand on Friday from Delhi to communicate this. So, on that day itself he got the keys of the company's office. On March 17, on the auspicious occasion of Gudi Padwa, New Year's Day as per the Hindu (Marathi) calendar, the company started its operations. Interestingly, Persistent was the first company to occupy the STP premises.

Anand used his personal savings of Rs 360,000 to kick-start the venture. The company also managed to get a loan of Rs 6 lakh from a public sector bank to meet its working capital requirements, but getting the loan was a challenging task. Due to the bad economic climate in the country, all bank loan applications were placed on hold in mid-1991. It took the company nearly six months to get the loan sanctioned.

ANAND'S TAKE ON START-UPS

'The biggest challenge that a small company faces is related to cash flows. We made sure that we were getting regular payments and it was collected on time. In fact, we structured the payment schedule to ensure that we could manage cash flows well and though we were compromising a little bit on earnings, we ensured that there was a steady cash flow for salaries and other expenses.'

The company focused on outsourced software product development. Even though it was a norm for Indian companies in those days to do the projects onsite, Persistent deliberately decided against this. In the early 1990s, communication was very difficult and expensive. Every morning, the Persistent team would connect to CompuServe to download mails and would send mails by uploading them in the evening. They had to keep a record of the number of bytes transferred. Speed was very slow, just 2400 bps to 9600 bps. They would chunk messages in 30 K byte files and it took about five to six minutes to upload each such file. 'It was actually cheaper to go to Mumbai and check mails. I had a second class Deccan Queen express train pass which cost Rs 180 per month. I would go to Mumbai every Thursday, which was our weekly off, just to check mails!'

Importing computers was also not an easy task. The US government had stringent export control laws. It took the company almost three months to import its first computer, which had an Intel 486 microprocessor, as the company was required to get an export clearance from the US.

The company got its third client, Microsoft, in 1992, which proved be a turning point. It came at a very critical time, when Persistent was struggling. It was a fairly small project—to migrate graphics libraries from 16 bit assembly to 32 bit, but this order proved significant for the company. Thereafter, every time somebody asked about its offshore capability, the company showed them a letter from Microsoft commending it on having delivered to its requirements.

Anand stresses that the ability to hire peers is the most critical item in the success of a company, especially when constituting the core team. Getting talented people was a very hard task in the initial years. 'Nobody likes to join a small company. Instead, everyone prefers a brand name. When we were hiring, we would tell people that at Persistent they would get to work on new things that were in demand and that would improve their résumé.'

Persistent was one of the first companies in India to introduce Employee Stock Ownership Plans (ESOPs) and a good percentage of the company is held under these. This was its way of giving back to employees—having employees own the company and participate in its success. It's not unusual in the US, where most of its customers are based, and the company was inspired by them in adopting these kinds of best practices.

In the initial years, Anand was pretty much a programmer in the company. He looked at this as a profession more than a business, and wanted to stay on the technical side by conscious choice. In 1997–98, on the advice of his colleagues, he decided to shift focus to the sales and product delivery part of the business.

Persistent took nine long years to reach a figure of hundred people, in the year 1999. The company, till then, had focused only on very specialized technical work. The team ran Persistent as a boutique firm and did only esoteric projects at that time.

Intel Capital invested $1 million in Persistent in 2000, triggering the company to grow to a strength of 500 employees in 2003. The reason for this was that the company, by that time, had added services that supported the entire life cycle of product development. The team used the analogy of the Honda Motor company to reassure themselves that they were doing the right thing. Honda started out as a bicycle engine manufacturing company, and grew to build motorcycle engines, car engines, and then began to manufacture cars. They paralleled the company's transition of growing from a boutique shop building core database technology components in 1990 to being responsible for the entire product, to Honda's transition from an engine manufacturer to a car manufacturer. While this transition took place, Honda continued to focus on its core expertise in building engines and continues to be the leader in the automobile engines market.

Norwest Venture Partners and Gabriel Venture Partners, two venture capital firms, invested a total of Rs 85 crore in Persistent in 2005. The employee strength crossed 6300 in 2010–11. The company is working in diverse areas like telecommunications, life sciences, healthcare, and banking. Since 2010, the company has also invested in new technology areas such as cloud computing, mobility, analytics, and enterprise collaboration. Anand believes that these technology areas are set to redefine the market and sees companies like Persistent playing a vital role in delivering efficient, cost-effective, and reduced time-to-market products. The target to get a significant percentage of the business beyond engineering products, according to Anand, is still under way.

ANAND'S ACHIEVEMENTS

In recognition of his contribution to the IT sector, Anand was awarded the Entrepreneur Award at the Brihan Maharashtra Mandal Convention held in Atlanta in 2005. He is also the recipient of the CSI Fellowship Award 2007 for Outstanding Achievement in the Field of Information Technology. He was awarded the Career Achievement Award from the School of Informatics at Indiana University, Bloomington, in 2009, and serves on the Dean's Advisory Council at the same university.

Anand is currently the co-convener for Association of Computing Machinery (ACM) India Council and a member of the executive committee of NASSCOM.

Anand indulged in things that he liked doing. That's why he feels Persistent has had a very different growth trajectory. 'It is always hard to compare, and you can't always compare different companies—because situations are different and what they do is different. We had our own values and we wanted to do business in a particular way. When you choose to work in a particular way, sometimes you will need to face constraints, but that you have to live with.' In the initial years, Persistent was among the few companies that had initiated flexible time and hours option for employees.

Anand gives us a beautiful insight into his leadership skills. 'While working on a customer's project, we lost some business just because we were not willing to provide support for products. Losing business is not good. So next

time onwards we set out to find out what resources it would take to do it and we started creating cases where we could implement that.'

In March 2010, the IPO of the company got a tremendous response from the investors and was oversubscribed 93 times. Anand feels that the scope for growth is very large if one looks at what's happening in the market. More and more products are being built. If one looks at how the world is moving, people are trying to assemble more complete products rather than custom-built software. **'So, the product business is definitely going to grow; in fact, it will be much bigger than the market for building application software in the future,'** he says.

Anand considers himself fortunate to have founded the company with his father. In 1990, his father had just retired and, having enough free time, he helped Anand out. Gradually, he got quite involved in the company. Anand's father focused on the non-technical aspects and served as Executive Director till 2009. Anand considers his father his mentor.

Persistent is a company well respected for its corporate social responsibility (CSR). Since 1993, it has been donating about 1 percent of its profits to social causes. To institutionalize the CSR initiative of the company and develop a systematic approach to administering the process of donations, Persistent formed a public charitable trust called Persistent Foundation in 2008–09. The Foundation is primarily involved in the three key areas of healthcare, education, and community development.

Some of the unique initiatives the company has taken include the setting up of the Pune Cyber Lab for Pune Police, in collaboration with NASSCOM, to provide training to the police force. The company has also supported the Science Exploratory at Bharatiya Vidya Bhavan in Pune. The company has been a part of an exciting industry–academia programme with the Inter University Center for Astronomy and Astrophysics (IUCAA). The company has jointly established the Virtual Observatory India which is a part of an international programme that has allowed observatories to exchange data which is of immense value to Indian astronomers.

Truly, Persistent Systems has lived up to its name. 'Persistent systems' is a technical term used for systems that are persistent on the computer's disk. Databases are typically 'persistent systems' and since the team started out by building database systems, Persistent Systems clearly denoted their focus.

Persistent Systems is on a roll; it is expanding into different domains, people, and geographies, and having a lot of fun in the process.

ANAND'S SUCCESS TIPS

- Be persistent.

- Just do it! That's the main thing. When you choose to act, things happen.

- There will always be issues. Things will always go wrong. However, you have to come back the next day, sit, think, and keep moving.

AGENT OF CHANGE

Arvind Kejriwal

Nehru Hall, 1989
India Against Corruption (Member)

This man in trousers and a shirt with a Reynolds pen in his shirt pocket, resembles a typical government clerk. He keeps a black moustache, travels by the Metro, and has no qualms sleeping on the floor of railway platforms.

A former bureaucrat with the Indian Revenue Service, Arvind Kejriwal has already created a revolution with the Right to Information (RTI) movement in the country through his organization Parivartan. He is a key member of India Against Corruption, a citizens' movement that demands strong anti-corruption laws.

NANNU, A MIDDLE AGED daily wage earner from an east Delhi slum, lost his ration card which provided his family cheap grain and other essential commodities from India's public distribution system (PDS). He applied for a duplicate ration card in January 2004. According to the rules he should have got his ration card within ten days, but for three months he kept running around in vain. The government officers were expecting a bribe. He didn't have the money to pay the bribe and often he was not even allowed to enter the local Food and Civil Supplies Office because he was shabbily dressed. His family and friends knew that it was no use. Nothing will change, this is India. *Is desh ka kuch nahin ho sakta.* These are the feelings that come to everyone's mind when one sees injustice meted out to a fellow citizen. This attitude of people is very difficult to change.

However, Nannu approached Parivartan, the brainchild of Arvind Kejriwal. Parivartan encouraged him to file a Right to Information (RTI) application questioning why he was being denied a ration card. On the fourth day after submitting the application, the food inspector came to his house to inform him that his card was ready. When he went to collect his card, the Food and Supply Officer, who is the head of a district, escorted him to his office room, offered him tea, gave him his card, and requested him to take back his application under the RTI Act. Nannu, who had been running around for three months and was a persona non grata in the eyes of those officers, had suddenly become a VIP! Now you can find this illiterate, confident man helping others file RTI applications.

One might think that Arvind must have been an activist in his schooldays, but he was actually a bookworm. He did nothing else but study.

This son of an engineer came all the way from the little town of Hissar in Haryana to IIT Kharagpur in 1985 to pursue Mechanical Engineering. He was amazed to see people speaking in English but quickly grappled with the inferiority complex he suffered. At IIT, Arvind enjoyed his life, actively participating in cultural activities and winning numerous awards. His Hindi debating skills were readily acknowledged in the campus. Arvind, known as 'Kejri' to his friends in IIT, excelled in Hindi dramatics as well. '**IIT has contributed immensely to my personality and I give the entire credit to it for whatever I am today.**'

After graduating from IIT in 1989, Arvind joined Tata Steel in Jamshedpur. He recalls that it was a time when nearly 80 to 90 percent of an IIT batch used to go abroad. He knew even back then that he wanted to do something for society.

Arvind sat for the Civil Services Examination and qualified for the Indian Revenue Service (IRS) in 1992. To get into the much coveted Indian Administrative Service, he made another attempt at the examination, and before the results were declared he travelled extensively around India. He went into the interiors of the insurgency-hit Bodoland and other areas of the North East. His stint with Mother Teresa's Missionaries of Charity in Kolkata for two months was a complete eye-opener. He saw a lot of poverty, sick people on footpaths, some even with gangrene. Subsequently, he joined the Ramakrishna Mission in Kolkata and then travelled all across Haryana by joining the Nehru Yuva Kendra.

He began to realize how backward these parts of India were. But he still had no answers then as to what holds back a community from development. What he did have was a whole set of questions.

Results were declared and this time too his rank fetched him the IRS only. So Arvind joined the IRS in 1993. After his training, he was posted at the Income Tax Commissioner's Office in Delhi in 1995 as Assistant Commissioner.

He recounts that often chartered accountants would casually ask him if they could 'do something for me', which he would politely refuse and show them the door. In a few months, his reputation as an honest officer was established and the offers stopped coming. He didn't even keep a peon and used to clean up the office room himself.

'While serving in the IRS I realized the kind of power the bureaucracy enjoys. It's too much and there is absolutely no accountability and transparency. This has led to inefficiency and wanton corruption. The problem is the lack of transparency,' he says.

Gradually, Arvind realized that he couldn't do much against corruption while being in the bureaucracy. In January 2000, with a few friends, he formed Parivartan (which means 'change' in Hindi), a Delhi-based citizens' movement to work on ensuring just, transparent, and accountable governance. Its aim was to provide relief to the people who do not want to pay bribes but are forced to pay them. Arvind calls this 'extortionist' bribery and says, '**Every single individual in the country is subject to this form of bribery in some form or the other.**'

Arvind's job had given him an insight into the bureaucratic system at the Income Tax Department. Hence, that was Parivartan's first target. Arvind started working under pseudonyms to avoid the complications that might arise from his seniors and colleagues.

In the Income Tax Department, tax refunds and PAN allotments were being deliberately delayed in expectation of bribes. The Parivartan team met the Chief Income Tax Commissioner to inform him that they would bring to him cases where bribes were being sought, to which he agreed. They also appealed to him to implement a few simple suggestions to make the department transparent. They put up banners across Delhi which read, '**Don't pay bribes in the Income Tax Department. If you have a problem, contact Parivartan. We will get your work done free of cost.**' Now, the Commissioner berated them for putting up banners that implied that his department was corrupt. Despite that, cases through them got solved on the strength of numbers. The print media too published a few cases and they petitioned the Public Accounts Committee and the Chief Vigilance Commissioner, adding pressure on the department. But the suggestions for transparency never got implemented.

Parivartan filed a Public Interest Litigation (PIL) in the Delhi High Court in July 2000, seeking to direct the department to implement the suggestions. Arvind went on leave from his IRS job from November 2000. Manish Sisodia, a Parivartan member and a journalist, got the media to cover the campaign. The department reluctantly filed an affidavit in April 2001 that directions had been issued for the implementation of the suggestions. However, no such direction was ever issued. In July 2001, thirty volunteers of Parivartan sat in a peaceful protest in the corridor outside the Commissioner's office. This forced him to implement the reforms.

From August 2000, Arvind, a Gandhian, had stationed himself along with other Parivartan members outside some of the offices of the Delhi Vidyut Board (DVB)—the electricity department—every day during public dealing hours. They would exhort visitors not to pay bribes and offered to facilitate their dealings with the department free of cost. Seven families in Maujpur had been running from pillar to post to get a new electricity connection through DVB since 1994. Each family was asked to shell out Rs 5000 as bribe. They approached Parivartan in October 2000 and quickly got the new connections.

The Parivartan members felt that people were coming to depend on the organization without being empowered themselves. Arvind realized that while his efforts may have considerably eliminated middlemen and touts and the chances of bribery, 'we too were acting as brokers, albeit honest brokers'.

Accidentally, Arvind came across the Delhi RTI Act in late 2001, in a small newspaper report. 'We took a copy of the law which had been passed just then, studied it and found that it could be a very powerful tool. What we found was that earlier we had been acting as middlemen and were struggling with what to do. RTI provided us with the answer.'

To know how the law worked, Parivartan filed some dummy applications in departments like the Municipal Corporation of Delhi (MCD) and DVB. Arvind was shocked to know that these departments were not even aware that such a law had been passed. Parivartan gave the officials copies of the law. This didn't work, so Parivartan wrote a letter to the chief minister. The chief minister called a meeting of all the departments in January 2002 and directed them to implement the law.

Parivartan's first success story under the RTI Act was scripted in February 2002. A citizen, Ashok Gupta, had been unable to get a new electricity connection for the last two years because he refused to pay a bribe of Rs 5000. As per the rules, a consumer is supposed to receive his electricity connection within thirty days of applying. Instead of taking up his complaint with the department, Parivartan asked him to file an application under the RTI Act. He submitted the RTI application which Parivartan drafted, and within ten days his work was done. It was almost miraculous. '**After this we stopped taking grievances from people and the focus shifted to raising awareness and increasing participation. Within three months we helped 300 people file RTI applications and everyone got their jobs done in ten to fifteen days, some of which had been pending for several years!**'

The MCD was the last department to implement RTI. On March 3, 2003, Parivartan organized a dharna outside the office of the Additional Commissioner and submitted an application to implement RTI. The Additional Commissioner said that MCD was a big department and needed time to implement. The Parivartan members told him that they would again come back after two months and would keep sitting until RTI was implemented. Under pressure, the MCD implemented RTI.

Parivartan had its office in a slum called Sundernagri in east Delhi. Under the RTI Act they obtained copies of all the contracts given by MCD in the last two years in the area. Out of 168 contracts, they shortlisted 68 and verified them. They went from street to street. '**We would beat drums and collect people and tell them about the government schemes and the work that was supposed to have been done in their colony in the last two years. We asked them about the actual work done,**' says Arvind.

Urban India's first ever Jan Sunvayi—public hearing—was held on December 14, 2002 in Sundernagri. Around 1000 to

1500 people gathered. A panel chaired by a former Supreme Court judge was formed. MCD officials were present and the local MLA came. Actual work done from each of the contracts was read out. It was found that of the 68 contracts worth Rs 1.3 crore, items worth Rs 70 lakh were missing; 59 hand pumps were claimed to be installed but only 14 were found; 29 electric motors were supposed to have been installed, but not a single motor could be seen on the spot. There were some roads which were shown to have been made two to three times within six months but had not been made even once. A detailed report was prepared and submitted to the Chief Minister and the Municipal Commissioner. There was no action taken. So Parivartan finally filed a PIL in the Delhi High Court on the basis of which the police were directed to register an FIR.

Due to the buzz created by the Jan Sunvayi, many people came forward with their complaints about the PDS to Parivartan.

Triveni Devi had a meagre family income, with less than Rs 500 coming in per month. The ration shop at Sundernagri kept denying Triveni her quota of wheat and rice month after month. However, after six months, she approached Parivartan and filed an RTI application forcing the ration shop owner to reveal the records. According to the books, 25 kg of wheat and 10 kg of rice were purportedly being issued to her every month and the cash memos even had her fake thumb impressions. Triveni was a literate woman and could actually sign. But before she could do anything, the shopkeeper begged her for forgiveness.

The area had almost 10,000 families and seventeen shops catering to them. Parivartan asked for records from all seventeen shops. '**At that time all the officers and shopkeepers came together and refused to give the records**,' Arvind says. Parivartan continued the battle for transparency in the dealings of ration shops for the next two years and the case even went to the Delhi High Court which directed that the records be given. '**Records were burnt, Parivartan members were beaten up. In the area, over 90 percent of the grain ration was being skimmed off by shopkeepers in collusion with the food department officials**,' he says.

Nineteen-year-old Santosh, a girl from the slums of Sundernagri, worked for Parivartan and was a great street organizer. On December 29, 2004 her throat was slashed by a shopkeeper. Thankfully, after several days of struggle, she survived. After this incident, which was the seventh attack on them, Parivartan members seriously thought whether they could continue these campaigns. Family members of the girl put pressure on her to quit Parivartan and get married. Despite this Santosh was undeterred and said, '**We can't stop like this. I have to do something to improve my country. No one is going to come from America or Japan.**' Finally, the Delhi government took notice and issued orders to clean up the PDS. Parivartan had finally won a two-year-long battle.

In November 2004, Arvind came across a newspaper report about the Delhi government's decision to privatize water supply. After six months' struggle, Parivartan obtained 10,000 pages of communication under the RTI Act between government agencies and the World Bank, which was funding the project. The records revealed that the World Bank had manipulated the bidding for a contract to plan the privatization. The team sent the documents to professors of IIM Ahmedabad and IIM Bengaluru, who held a press conference in Delhi. Pamphlets were distributed across Delhi. The project would have hiked tariffs tenfold and cut off free supply of water to the city's poor. Parivartan's efforts successfully stalled the project.

October 12, 2005 was a red letter day in the history of India, as the central RTI act came into force, heralding a new era in governance. Every citizen in the country now possessed the right to inspect government documents. Arvind says that it's the only law in the country after Independence which related the performance of government officers to their salary. If they did not provide information within thrity days the officers' salary would be deducted.

Arvind was a part of the team that drafted the law. The law lays down the machinery to use our fundamental right to information. Arvind says that this was not a charity given away by the government but the culmination of a long-drawn movement started by the poorest sections of society way back in 1990 in Rajasthan under the leadership of Aruna Roy.

ARVIND ON THE IMPORTANCE OF RTI

'The RTI is crucial because every citizen in this country pays tax. Even a beggar on the street pays tax while buying a bar of soap or a matchbox. These taxes collected by the government, including from the poorest of the poor, belong to us. We are the masters and the government servants exist to serve us. It is the duty of every master to take accounts from the servant from time to time, but we the masters of the country never took any accounts from our government since Independence.'

To spread the message of RTI across the country, the 'Drive against bribe campaign' was conducted from July 1 to July 15, 2006. Parivartan partnered with NGOs across the country and got over 1500 volunteers across fifty-five cities. With the help of media houses, a call was given to the nation that there was no need to pay bribes; they could use the RTI instead. Help centres were set up. Almost 22,000 people filed their RTI applications, which was more than the number of applications filed since the RTI Act came into existence.

Arvind was honoured with the prestigious Ramon Magsaysay Award in 2006 for fighting corruption. However, Arvind says that the award does not belong to him, rather, it belongs to the entire RTI movement and every RTI activist in the country.

With IRS batchmate turned wife Sunita and two children

for moral support, Arvind has led his crusade against corruption with full vigour.

Arvind quit as Additional Commissioner of Income Tax in February 2006. He took full advantage of the long leaves that his job permitted. For him the decision of resigning was an evolving process, but not a comforting decision for his middle-class family as it reduced their financial security.

Arvind donated the $50,000 Magsaysay Award prize money to set up the Public Cause and Research Foundation (PCRF) in December 2006. The foundation has instituted National RTI awards to honour the people who have kept the flag of RTI flying high: public information officers, information commissioners, and citizens alike. 'We wanted to create a positive reinforcement, so that the good officers would be encouraged to give information.'

There is no doubt that the RTI has ushered in a transparency revolution. However, do people have control over their life and destiny or are they still in the hands of bureaucrats and politicians?

In ancient and medieval India, almost all decisions were taken in gram sabhas—the village assemblies. During the time of Gautama Buddha, though rulers were not elected and the king's son would succeed his father, the day-to-day decisions of governance were taken in village assemblies. The decisions of village assemblies were respected by the king. The British replaced this by the collector system and all the powers were vested with bureaucrats. Mahatma Gandhi believed that every village should be a republic unto itself. Arvind says that unfortunately at the time of Independence the British system was not replaced with the older, Indian model. Currently, people elect their representatives once in five years. Thereafter, they have no say in governance, except pleading with their representatives.

This led Arvind to launch the 'Swaraj Abhiyan', a movement for citizens' rule. Swaraj means giving direct control of funds, functions, and functionaries to people's assemblies. These assemblies should meet every month.

In Delhi, the Abhiyan is encouraging people to form their own mohalla sabhas. Several mohalla sabhas have started functioning and the results are very encouraging. Here, the people, government officers, and councillors come together and chalk down priorities on how their funds should be utilized, and payments are not made to contractors until people are satisfied with the work. But there is a need for a law to institutionalize the mohalla sabhas. Similarly, the Abhiyan is targeting villages across the country and urging people to force their sarpanchs to take decisions in gram sabhas only. This decentralization of power will ensure that people have a say in day-to-day governance.

While Arvind was engaged in the Swaraj Abhiyan, Delhi proudly hosted the Commonwealth Games in October 2010. However, even before the Games, the widespread corruption involved in the preparation brought disrepute to the country and infuriated the people. With time, his dissatisfaction with the implementation of the RTI Act had grown. PCRF's research found out that politicians and bureaucrats had found loopholes in the Act to hide information. The RTI helped unearth scams, but the culprits were roaming free in most of the cases. RTI activists were being threatened with dire consequences and a few were even murdered. The lack of an effective independent investigative agency in a country where bribes are an accepted norm was the culprit, Arvind realized. '**There is zero risk in corruption and it's a high-profit business.**'

Arvind mobilized many social activists under the banner of India Against Corruption (IAC) to draft a citizens' version of the Lokpal Bill called the Jan Lokpal Bill. Huge public consultations took place to improve the bill. The IAC conducted public awareness drives in a big way to campaign for the bill.

THE JAN LOKPAL BILL

The Lokpal Bill was first introduced in Parliament in 1968 and the tenth time in 2008, but these various versions never got passed. The aim of the Jan Lokpal Bill is to effectively deter corruption, redress citizens' grievances and protect whistle-blowers. An independent ombudsman body called the Lokpal would be formed if the bill is made into a law. The Lokpal would be empowered to register and investigate corruption complaints against bureaucrats and politicians without prior government approval.

ARVIND'S ACHIEVEMENTS

Arvind was given the Magsaysay Award in 2006 for 'activating India's right-to-information movement at the grassroots, empowering Delhi's poorest citizens to fight corruption by holding government answerable to the people'.

For the extensive number of social causes he has been working on, Arvind was awarded the Ashoka Fellowship in 2004 for civic engagement, the Satyendra K. Dubey Memorial Award by IIT Kanpur in 2005 for his campaign for bringing transparency in government, the CNN-IBN Indian of the Year in the Public Service category for the year 2006, the NDTV Indian of the Year 2011, and the Global PanIIT Award in 2011. He was honoured with the coveted Distinguished Alumnus Award by IIT Kharagpur in 2009.

Due to the Union Government's indifferent attitude to the Jan Lokpal Bill, Gandhian Anna Hazare sat on an indefinite fast at Jantar Mantar in Delhi in April 2011. Respecting public opinion, the government agreed to form a joint drafting committee, comprising union ministers and members of the IAC, which included Arvind, to draft an effective Lokpal Bill.

The drafting committee exercise was a failure and the government introduced its own version of the bill in Parliament on August 4, 2011.

The IAC termed it a 'toothless bill'. Hazare sat on a fast from August 16, the day following the country's Independence

Day. He and Arvind, along with some other activists, were arrested and sent to Tihar Jail in Delhi. A huge public outcry forced the government to set them free. The fast continued at Delhi's Ramlila Maidan. The movement caught the imagination of the nation. Millions of people frustrated with unbridled corruption poured into the streets all over the country and even abroad, with Gandhi caps on their heads and the tricolour in their hands. This peaceful agitation, which struck a chord with the nation, heralded a new era.

Parliament passed a unanimous resolution on August 27 agreeing in principle to the Jan Lokpal Bill's salient points. Hazare broke his fast the next day, signalling the triumph of the people.

Now, Arvind wants to channelize the huge public support the movement garnered to usher in electoral reforms in the country. These set of measures include the right to reject candidates fighting elections, the right to recall elected representatives, and involvement of gram sabhas in policy-making.

The soft-spoken, unassuming Arvind has a latent grit and fire that shines through as he speaks. A participatory democracy, which Arvind is vying for, will ensure that the state is accountable to the nation and the people.

ARVIND'S SUCCESS TIPS

- Have the will to act on your idea.

- Keep an eagle eye on your aim. Go after it with die-hard determination and full devotion.

- Be true to yourself and your morals. If you have the right morals, you will overcome any obstacle that stands in your path.

- Do contribute to society in whatever way you can. Take out some time for society. And don't make excuses about it.

LET THERE BE LIGHT

Dr H. Harish Hande

Nehru Hall, 1990
SELCO (Founder and Managing Director)

If you happen to be travelling through rural Karnataka, you'll see households twinkling in an ocean of darkness. What you would've witnessed is the impact of Harish Hande, SELCO, and their solar lanterns.

Harish Hande founded SELCO in 1995, and for the past sixteen years it has been changing the face of rural Karnataka and parts of Gujarat by providing sustainable solar energy.

'Rather than love, than money, than fame, give me truth.'

— Thoreau

TRUTH IS EXACTLY WHAT one gets from Harish Hande—the truth of the Bharat we live in and the truth of humanity. The truth hidden from urban India, what policymakers fail to see, and what many like to brush under the carpet.

One tends to think that Harish must have had some moving experience in his childhood that led him to such noble humanitarian deeds. On the contrary, Harish says, '**My childhood has nothing to do with it. I was born and brought up in the industrial town of Rourkela. I was pampered as a child and had no shortcomings.**'

Harish reckons that his first twenty-first days of orientation at IIT was the turning point. It changed the way he looked at life. He started doing new things which he had never done before in his life, such as playing hockey and debating, and met people from parts of India he'd never been to. Harish became conscious about society in his second year at IIT. Even his tenure as Hall President reflects this fact. '**My aim was to make the students socialize with each other. For me, the hostel represented the country.**' He never let students from the same state be roommates.

A student of Energy Engineering, Harish hobnobbed with some exceptional people such as Pavan Vaish, founder of Daksh, which was acquired by IBM. IIT armed Harish with the confidence and social awareness with which he was able to cross several hurdles. After leaving IIT, it was a succession of curious events which led to the creation of SELCO.

Harish did his master's and PhD from the University of Massachusetts, Lowell. His PhD days took Harish to a number of impoverished countries in Latin America. During his travels, he saw the dire poverty of people and the subhuman conditions that they lived in, and something stirred in him. He says, '**It made me forget which nationality I belonged to. All the divisions which society had created seemed meaningless. The battle shouldn't be between developed and developing nations but between the rich and the poor because that is the dichotomy of the situation. The suffering is the same for the poor in the US as it is in India.**' He feels that it is the poor who always suffer the most as they hardly get any electricity through conventional sources and end up paying the most for it. '**The poor have to part with 10 to 15 percent of their income to get a single light source. The rich don't pay that much for a single light.**'

In the Dominican Republic, Harish saw poor people effectively using solar energy. That particular experience affected him deeply and he changed his PhD thesis from Thermodynamics to Rural Electrification by Solar Energy. To test solar sustainability in practice, he moved from the US to Sri Lanka to complete his thesis.

Harish set up base in a village in northern Sri Lanka, where he stayed with a local family as a paying guest, and where he learned to live without electricity. Harish believes terrorism, like that perpetrated by the LTTE, is nothing but a by-product of poverty, and the lack of basic needs is what drives people to pick up arms. If the poor are empowered, they would definitely be able to sustain their livelihood. Thus, in 1993, Harish, with co-founder Neville Williams, conceptualized Solar Electric Light Company or SELCO, which went on to become a registered company in 1995.

The primary philosophy of SELCO is to provide reliable energy services at people's doorstep in rural India. SELCO believes that solar electricity can lead to a better quality of life. It can lead to increased savings by reducing the cost of fuels, and increased earnings as a result of the extra hours available for work. The model on which SELCO is based has a rather interesting story behind it.

A contact of Harish in the village told him about a rich areca nut farmer who could probably provide them with funds for their project. Harish went to him to explain the concept of solar lighting. The farmer heard Harish out but could not see the benefit of the solar lighting and dismissed him. The farmer's 70-year-old mother, however, had listened to the conversation and she came forward. She asked Harish to not talk, but to show her son how this idea worked. She gave him Rs 15,000 to secretly install the system on her son's field. Harish and his team set it up in three and a half hours and left.

When night fell, the son saw his field lit up and was amazed by it. '**It was that old lady who had established our business model— "demonstrate the benefit instead of talking"**,' says Harish. In fourteen years, that model has not changed.

SELCO started with just four technicians—class 4 dropouts who worked in television repair shops. Harish found them during his travels in villages. According to Harish, they were the pillars of SELCO. '**Education breeds insecurity, I was worried whether SELCO would take off. Those four people worked for almost no pay and had more faith in SELCO than anyone else, including me. They gave me boundless confidence.**' After a few years, he met a lot of people who liked SELCO's concept and joined in at senior positions.

Here's an overview of how SELCO uses sustainable solar energy to the advantage of the poor. Take the example of a group of tribal people in ninety-eight homes, where five to six families lived in each house. They were day labourers working in somebody else's fields. They rolled bidis at night under small kerosene lights to make extra money. They told Harish that was all they could do because kerosene light illuminated only a small area. Harish's group asked them what they would do if they had more light, and the group said that they were very good basket makers and could make two to three baskets a night instead, for Rs 30 each. He asked them whether they would be willing to give Rs 5 per basket to pay for the light, and they were more than delighted to do so. Harish's group connected the labourers to somebody who was willing to buy the baskets made by these families. The clients paid Rs 5 per basket for the loan, and in four years they had paid off the loan for the lighting. That is, they had to pay Rs 300 per month to SELCO for the solar lighting, and in return, were able to make an additional profit of Rs 1500. This scheme involved some basic arithmetic and understanding the thought process of the villagers. It's a complete contradiction to the popular belief that solar energy is too expensive for the poor.

SELCO'S ACHIEVEMENTS

Since its inception, SELCO has installed twenty-five energy centres in the two states, Karnataka and Gujarat, and offers a variety of energy services to more than 120,000 households. SELCO has been able to convert the powerless common man into a self-sustained micro-entrepreneur.

What SELCO essentially does is to assess the energy requirements of the customer, then buy the appropriate solar products, be it lighting appliances, inverters, heaters, or cooking stoves. The equipment is financed by the bank, which requires some initial down payment. This is where SELCO steps in and pays the amount as a guarantee. Over the years, the company has tied up with organizations such as the Global Village Energy Partnership and United Nations Environment Programme to finance the down payment to SELCO. Customers are able to pay the money back in easy instalments.

The primary secret behind Harish's success has been his utter disregard of class hierarchy which society imposes on everyone. According to him, to really understand the problems of the poor, you have to be one of them. This is an example of his disregard for class structure. They were in Mangalore for a seventeen-day village exhibition. Harish would sleep on the site for the safety of their system, unlike the owners of other stalls who left their workers behind. The other workers thought he was a worker as well and treated him as one of them. They became close friends and would speak their hearts out to each other. On the last two days, some of Harish's friends from the US as well as some government officers came to meet him. The workers, realizing the differences in background, went up to Harish and apologized. '**I felt I had lost eighteen of my close friends that day due to this stupid class structure**,' says Harish. Even in his office, Harish preaches a 'no door' concept where anyone can speak his or her mind and be blunt about it. '**When someone in the organization feels that I have made a mistake, he or she can come into my room and say, "Harish, this is wrong", and leave without giving me a chance to answer.**'

All was not smooth sailing, though, for SELCO. Starting off in an uncharted territory like solar energy in those days was pretty difficult from an investment point of view. There was no concept of venture capital in India and investors were not easily convinced about funding a project which was not a proven technology. Harish initially had to sustain the company on his paltry PhD scholarship fund, which had some Rs 15,000 left in it, enough to buy only one solar home lighting system. However, Harish thinks the lack of funds worked in SELCO's favour. **'SELCO became more innovative due to our lack of funds. Today, financial innovation is our forte. It's actually nothing but pure mathematics and logic. People say we think out of the box, but it's just a case of not knowing what's in the box. If a banker tells me a proposed thing can't be done, I ask for five different possible paths to go around the problem. We never take no for an answer, and we look for all possible alternatives and choose the best possible solution.'**

In 1996, Malaprabha Grameena Bank financed 100 of their systems, which was a breakthrough, and soon, other banks followed suit. Today, SELCO is in a position to pick and choose their options in terms of investors and partners. They have raised $2 million since the early days. They broke even in 2000, were profitable till 2005, but suffered losses for the following three years. Ironically, this was due to a few policy changes in the European market. Since 2009–10, they have become profitable again.

Another thing that played to Harish's advantage was his age. He entered the solar industry very early. When he went to solar conferences, Harish was a child among old men. People were excited to see a young kid, so they gave him all kinds of advice and passed on information rather than telling him to learn from experience. They were passionate people who taught him history. They had met and known legends like Mahatma Gandhi and Martin Luther King. They taught him the most important thing in life—passion.

SELCO has been able to benefit from the policy of carbon credits as they help in displacing kerosene. '**All our carbon credits have been sold out till 2012. What we do is considered "sexy", since we have photographs of children studying at night under solar lamps.**' According to Harish, terms like 'climate change' and 'global warming' are all meaningless. He thinks that if you were to address poverty, all other issues will be solved. And the method proposed for the alleviation of poverty is non-conventional sustainable energy. Harish does not assume that solar energy is 'the' solution. One has to mix and match energy sources according to situations. For example, a coastal region needs to harness wind as an energy solution rather than rely on solar power. To him, empowerment is the key to this issue. '**The generation of energy and use of fuel should be in the hands of the people, so they have a choice about its usage. This is what sustainable energy provides you with.**'

Harish believes that the government can play an important role in pushing the issue of sustainable energy. '**It can start off by passing appropriate policies, such as removing meaningless tax structures which exist in solar technology. There are huge subsidies in kerosene, which should be reduced as kerosene is harmful to the environment.**' Harish has had a complex relationship with the government, and feels that its interference could only harm SELCO and its customers. He says, 'It's kind of ironical that I have more influence on higher-ups in the UK and US rather than in my own country.'

HARISH AND SELCO'S ACHIEVEMENTS

Harish and SELCO received the Outstanding Achievement Award from Ashden Awards in 2007, the World's Leading Green Energy Award from Prince Charles in 2005, the Financial Times Boldness Award in 2008, the Social Entrepreneur of the Year Award in 2007 by the Schwab Foundation, and the Nand and Jeet Khemka Foundation Award, and the prestigious Ramon Magsaysay Award in 2011. In 2008, Harish was chosen by *Business Today* as one of the twenty-one young leaders for India's 21st century.

Harish wants SELCO to reach people of other states in India and also in other countries. However, his idea of scaling up is a bit different—going deeper into the economic strata. 'If we are serving people who earn Rs 3000 a month, then we would like to serve people earning Rs 1500.'

According to him, SELCO cannot grow to other states; it has to start from scratch everywhere as every state is different from the other, with its own traditions and culture. For SELCO to run in other states, it has to be run by a local person. SELCO in Maharashtra has to be run by a Maharashtrian. SELCO has set up its own incubation centre, where people can come and stay for months to work and learn from SELCO. This incubation centre is open to not only Indians but to people across the world. In the last five years about 100 students from institutes like MIT, Imperial, etc. have visited SELCO. Incidentally, SELCO is known more outside India than within the country itself. If one was to walk the corridors of MIT and ask them about SELCO, they would definitely know all about it.

SELCO has so far been pretty successful in whatever they have done in Karnataka. Harish thinks that if they had more competition, it would have brought out the best out of them; if there is no competition then there is a monopoly, and it's the worst possible thing for the poor. The poor need to have a choice. Competition should be looked upon as a partnership because your competitor will think of solutions and new innovations that may not have struck you. It is the best outcome for the poor. However, sometimes competition can fail. Shell had come to buy out SELCO, but they refused. So they set up a competition to SELCO. It collapsed miserably because they couldn't understand the needs of the people they were serving. Another disadvantage of not having competition is that they have to explain the product again and again. Since, there are no other players, people are sceptical about the technology.

Harish is proud to have a hardworking and passionate team of 170 people working with him. In SELCO, merit is given utmost importance. The current chief technician joined as an

---

HARISH'S TAKE ON THE MANY AWARDS SELCO HAS WON

'Let me make it clear, when SELCO initially applied for awards, it was just for money. There was no better place to find unrestricted money. When banks refused us loans, we used this money as a guarantee. Awards don't matter one bit to us. We never do a press release when we win an award.'

However, Harish is candid enough to admit that these awards have expanded their global network and they have utilized it. 'It is due to these awards that we have personally come to know influential people like Al Gore, and have been able to influence a lot of policies.'

---

office boy, and, because of his commitment, rose through the ranks. To them, a résumé doesn't matter; it is the motivation and the passion that really counts. At SELCO, both chartered accountants and scientists, who have settled for salaries much lower than the market, walk the same corridors. And, SELCO hires employees from the villages it works in. This helps them to understand their customers, and at the same time, builds trust. Nearly 80 percent of SELCO's employees are rural technicians. '**People in rural areas may lack money, but they are not short on talent. Villagers don't need help, they just need appropriate connections.**'

Harish bemoans the fact that there are very few educated Indians who are devoting themselves to giving back to society. '**It is really sad to see that the only competition I have in the solar industry in India is from three Stanford graduates.**'

Whenever he wins an award, he is quick to emphasize that it isn't he who has won it, it is SELCO. However, it's not these laurels which illustrate the change he has brought about in rural Karnataka. It is the prosperity that SELCO has brought to the destitute masses of the state and that preconceptions that Harish has shattered, which underline the greatness of this man.

HARISH'S SUCCESS TIPS

- Leave your computers, come out of your rooms, and interact with people. Talk, discuss, because that is how your management and negotiation skills develop, along with your ability to take criticism.

- Think a problem through and don't settle for a quick fix. Squeeze the lemon dry to get an additional drop or two out of it.

- Never be afraid to admit that you don't know something.

- While starting up, create a team to reduce the burden on your shoulders.

- If you want to be a successful social entrepreneur, you shouldn't run after funding or the media to get your story out. Let them come to you. If they do, you can rest assured that you have created a sustainable model.

- Finally, and most importantly, the ego must be eliminated. The moment you run after material wealth or think that you have achieved greatness, it will spell a downfall for you.

THE LADY MEANS BUSINESS

Anuradha Acharya

SN Hall, 1995
Ocimum Biosolutions (Founder and CEO)

Anuradha Acharya built her company, Ocimum Biosolutions, in the year 2000, when the fields of biotechnology and bioinformatics were in their infancy. She was just 28 years old.

Ocimum, a leading integrated global genomics company, is one of the top 25 pharmaceutical and biotechnology companies and leading research institutes worldwide among its clients.

ANURADHA ACHARYA'S USUAL loud laughter is a sign of the confidence she has in herself. However, behind this carefree façade lies an astute businesswoman.

Anu had the entrepreneurial streak in her right from her childhood. She says, '**My father encouraged the feeling of earning our living right from when we were children. He used to give us kids Rs 15 per month as pocket money and for other expenses, we had to earn it ourselves. He would pay us for small household chores, and I used to do as many as I could to earn more money, from painting chairs to ironing clothes. Those were some of my early brushes with entrepreneurship.**'

Anu grew up in the IIT Kharagpur campus where her father was a professor in the Department of Physics. Anu, too, wanted to be a physicist, and follow in her father's footsteps. In 1990, Anu's dream was realized and she was enrolled with the Department of Physics. It was quite an achievement for Anu as IITs have often faced criticism for the skewed gender ratio. In her batch of about 500 students, there were only ten girls! She recalls that she had a lot of fun on campus. '**I was an avid reader, which gave me the liberty to imagine a whole new world. I participated in a lot of cultural events, and played basketball and table tennis.**'

After completing her bachelor's, she enrolled herself in an integrated master's–PhD programme. However, she had a change of mind when she got bitten by the entrepreneurship bug. In 1995, she decided to leave the programme with just a master's degree and informed the head of the department about an alternative five-year plan. The plan envisaged her working for a small company, moving on to a larger company and finally starting her own company. This peculiar plan was meant for learning the tricks of the corporate world, a requisite for becoming an entrepreneur.

As per her plan, Anu armed herself with a master's each in Physics and Information Systems in 1997 from the University of Illinois, Chicago. Resisting the temptation of fat salaries offered to her by many big companies, she joined a start-up called Mantiss Information in the telecom sector in 1997. Here she was entrusted with the responsibility of a team leader, even though she had not done much computer programming till then.

Buoyed by the good experiences in the start-up, she joined a somewhat larger consulting firm called SEI Information in 1999, where she helped create a social networking site for entrepreneurs. She was perplexed by the palpable differences in the working culture in a start-up and a large company. At Mantiss, only optimization of work had mattered. However, at SEI, Anu spent her first fifty days just filling forms and doing mundane stuff.

All the while Anu had been thinking out ideas for her

own company. Many of the ideas were in the Internet, IT, and finance domains. Anu eventually chose the field of biotechnology because her friend Dr P. Sujata had expertise in biotechnology. Besides, biotechnology was an upcoming area and was hence less competitive. Back then, a search on Infoseek, a leading search engine, threw up just three entries for bioinformatics!

Ocimum Biosolutions came into existence in the year 2000, with an initial fund of Rs 7 lakh which came from the personal savings of the founders. Dr Sujata stayed back in the US to start the laboratory and Anu along with her IIT batchmate-turned-husband Subash returned to India to start the software unit. Hyderabad was the natural choice since it was where Anu's inlaws lived. In the US, while Anu was doing her master's, Subash was pursuing his MBA in Finance. The original plan was that the company would sequence medicinal plants in the US and the software unit in India would support the operations. The company would also generate intellectual property and offer some services to generate revenue. Ocimum is the botanical name for tulsi, or basil. Because they didn't want to limit themselves to sequencing, they added 'Biosolutions' to 'Ocimum' and named their company Ocimum Biosolutions.

The greatest asset for the company was its perfect founding team. Besides Anu, the team had a finance person in the form of Subash and a researcher in the form of Sujata. '**Having the right core team is essential because you alone can't have all** the requisite skills. It is not just about having a great idea. You need people who can sell it. If you can't sell your idea, it will never get converted into a successful venture,' says Anu.

The company started building software products to apply statistical methods that would help researchers in medical labs to collect and analyse the massive amounts of data generated. But very soon realization that India was not yet ready for biotechnology dawned on the team. From about 200 résumés received, Anu struggled to find someone fit enough. What came to the rescue of the company was the dotcom bubble burst. The global economy was reeling under economic recession, making it possible for Ocimum to hire some talented people who had worked in the US. To scale up, the company needed to hire more people. Anu came up with the idea of forming a training division in the company where people would be trained in IT and Life Sciences. This helped them develop talent and also meet revenue challenges. The company even collaborated with American universities to train people. Ocimum managed to train a few batches but when the company started getting criticized for being a 'training institute', it decided to discontinue its training programme.

Selling the first product is always a challenging, yet exciting experience for a new company. Ocimum faced an uphill task when in 2002 it sold its very first product, Biotracker, a laboratory information management system, in Hyderabad. It had just one month to deliver, and the promised product was yet to take concrete shape. '**Everybody stopped working** on other products. We worked day and night and delivered the product on the due date. Recreating those days now is not possible as then we had a very small team of just twenty people,' says Anu.

Anu's exemplary sales skills were reflected when Ocimum sold its gene optimization bioinformatics software, OptGene, to Dow AgroSciences in 2003. Dow was the client of a big company, so it was sceptical about using Ocimum's product. To win its confidence, Ocimum offered it a three-month trial at one-third the actual price. Half-heartedly, Dow accepted the offer. 'We would work throughout the day in India to incorporate the suggestions they gave us after using the software all through the day in the US. They sent us those suggestions in the morning, while it was actually the evening of the previous day in the US. So the time difference of 12 hours between the US and India worked to our advantage.' The final product was delivered at the end of three months and was a success. Interestingly, Dow continues to use the product even today. Ocimum not only showed what a good product it had, but also an unwavering commitment towards the client.

Anu followed a sales strategy she calls hard selling. As late as 2004, she would give product demonstrations to potential customers as a technical person. She would not even present her business card. That would instil much more confidence in customers when they later learnt that she was the founder. Her lack of background in biology was a major stumbling block.

Also her young age—she was not yet 30—was a barrier. She says, 'People generally don't take you seriously unless you have worked for about twenty years.'

The company collaborated with pharmaceutical and biotech research organizations, solving their challenges and increasing the productivity of their research and development efforts through the application of Ocimum's informatics expertise. Then it started licensing bioinformatics and enterprise software solutions like laboratory information management systems. From the third year itself, the company started making profit. The business was thriving and one could have been content with that. However, Anu had a vision that the company should become a 'lab next door' and not just be limited to bioinformatics. This meant that the company aspired to provide a researcher with services across the spectrum in a timely and cost-effective manner.

This vision led to an unconventional approach for a small company—the path of Mergers and Acquisitions (M&As). Ocimum had approached MWG Biotech of Germany in 2004 and was very close to signing a contract that would make MWG a customer. However, MWG began to struggle financially, and asked Ocimum to acquire its Genomic Diagnosis (GD) division. The business had failed and the asset being sold was in a bad state. But it had an impressive list of clients in Europe and the US, and a good foothold in microarray products. After due diligence, the acquisition took place in 2005, using Ocimum's internal funds and a small amount of bank debt. The company had a tough time dealing with unhappy MWG customers who had no idea what had happened to their projects as MWG faltered. That taught Anu a lesson—unhappy customers can be made happy if you engage them. If the company you are buying has current customers, make sure you reach out to them at the earliest possible moment.

The acquisition created a buzz which led to instant recognition and customer access worldwide for Ocimum. It began looking for its next target, a firm producing oligonucleotides. It found a likely target in Germany, but talks did not progress much before breaking down because the founder was unsure and also had a health problem. And another lesson was learnt—Ocimum had already made the announcement to its workforce that this deal was going ahead and having to retract that announcement was a challenge in managing both internal communications and morale.

Notwithstanding the setback suffered, Ocimum moved on to acquire Isogen Life Sciences based in the Netherlands in 2006. The plan was to expand Ocimum's European presence and sell oligonucleotides to research labs. The International Finance Corporation, the private equity arm of the World Bank, invested $6.5 million to make the acquisition possible. However, the acquisition was a failure. There was trouble with integration due to cultural issues, cost overruns, and intense competition that required a greater investment than originally anticipated. Even so, this merger helped Ocimum kick-start its new diagnostics division.

Gene Logic, a company based in Maryland, USA, was the next acquisition in 2007. Ocimum raised funds of $17 million from Kubera Cross-Border Fund (KUBC). Gene Logic had not only a database of disease-focused biomarker discovery and toxicogenomic suites it had built through dedicated microarray programmes, but also a fledgling services division. The database was difficult to replicate for competitors. Learning from the previous failure, Ocimum designed a perfect integration strategy. The team spent a fair amount of time with Gene Logic employees and hired external consultants. They retained Gene Logic's name to capitalize on the genomics goodwill associated with the brand.

Ocimum has created an entire genomics infrastructure all over the world, which can be used by anybody, ranging from an individual to academic institutions to large pharmaceutical companies. They can send their clinical samples to the company's labs, which are then stored in bio-repositories and bio-banks. Specific studies are conducted on them, data is analysed using the software tools the company has developed, and a report is sent back. The client, by outsourcing such procedures, can focus on core studies and is saved from the toil of setting up expensive labs. Thus Research as a Service (RaaS) offering from Ocimum helps pharmaceutical companies in reducing cost and time in drug discovery.

The company is now partnering with big pharmaceutical companies in the emerging field of personalized medicines, which is basically making medicines for an individual rather than for the masses. The company has so far filed for sixty-five patents in genomics and has over 300 highly skilled employees. It has annual revenue of over Rs 100 crore.

ANURADHA AND OCIMUM'S ACHIEVEMENTS

The World Economic Forum honoured Anuradha as the 2011 Young Global Leader. She was listed in the 25 Tech Titans under 35 by *Red Herring* magazine in 2006, named Biospectrum Entrepreneur of the Year in 2008, and awarded the Astia Life Science Innovators Award in the same year.

Ocimum has received several awards, including Fastest Growing Life Sciences Company in India by Red Herring Asia 100, and has been listed by Deloitte as one of the Fastest Growing Companies in Asia for four years in a row. The company was also given the IT Innovation Award 2005 by NASSCOM, which was presented by the then President of the country, Dr A.P.J. Abdul Kalam. Anu recalls that it was a memorable experience. In the few seconds on stage, Dr Kalam asked her to send the brochure of the company via email. 'Being an optimist, I sent him the email. Most amazingly, he replied within 24 hours asking for more information on microarray! On replying we got a purchase order from the Ministry of Defence!' She currently serves as a governing board member of the Council for Scientific and Industrial Research (CSIR) and at the National Institute for Biomedical Genomics (NIBMG).

Ocimum made headlines in May 2009 when it successfully developed an indigenous, relatively low-cost H1N1 Swine Flu detection kit. The same year the World Health Organization declared Swine Flu as a pandemic. The kit was affordable as it was made ten times cheaper than the imported ones.

What next? A billionaire? '**I am personally not interested in material wealth. I am more concerned about the growth of the company. We want to achieve certain milestones. We have plans of publicly listing the company in the coming years. We want to ensure that our employees feel proud about working in the company. We want to nurture the right set of people who can evolve with the changing needs of the company.**'

A woman running a business in India is quite uncommon because of the prevailing patriarchal notions. However, for Anu this was not an issue, and she credits her upbringing in the family for that. '**I was never treated as an inferior at home. It's only in the formative years when you may face this problem. If it happens later, you can deal with it. Only if you yourself have a problem in your mind would it become an issue.**'

Anu was once going through a *Forbes* article on the 100 richest Indians. Most men on the list were identified by their companies. However, the article mentioned every woman on the list by the name of her husband or father. The only exception was Kiran Mazumdar Shaw, the Chairperson of Biocon, and the article heaped praise on her by calling her India's richest self-made woman. Anu got a lot of help from

Kiran. She feels women now have role models to emulate. The times are changing as there are already quite a few women entrepreneurs running their companies and even more are emerging. Knowledge-based sectors such as biotechnology give a fair chance to women to leverage their advanced education and play a leadership role.

The biggest source of support for Anu is her husband Subash, a batchmate from IIT Kharagpur. **'We have been friends since 1991, and thereafter life partners and business partners, though technically, he reports to me! It is difficult to make all this work. We do all our "fighting" in our office. Yet, I know I have someone who is always there. We don't have defined roles and we interchange as and when required. That has always been an advantage for me.'**

Anu is the proud mother of two daughters, Neha who is 11 years old, and Akhila who is 4 years old. According to her, it is always challenging to balance the business and the family. **'I like spending a lot of time with my kids but I can't. Subash spends more time with them than I do. We try not to travel together to make sure that someone is there with the kids. We also make sure that we attend all their school functions and other events. My mother-in-law has also helped a lot in raising them.'** Such is Anu's dedication to Ocimum that she got back to work just two days after giving birth to her first child.

Big ideas, a dedicated team, lots of enthusiasm, and a never-say-die spirit is what Anu hopes to bank on as Ocimum consolidates its position in the life sciences world.

ANU'S SUCCESS TIPS

• You have to realize that entrepreneurship is not the glamorous job most people make it out to be. If you want to be an entrepreneur, you might not get much sleep, you might have to undergo a lot of pain and stress like constant travelling and meeting a lot of people. You will have to do a lot of things which you might not otherwise like to do.

• Entrepreneurship is not something that you do for a day or two. It is a very long term commitment, so brace yourself for it.

• Business is a constantly evolving thing, and you must have the appetite for variability and risk taking. If you like the security of a 9 to 5 high paying job then maybe this is not the right thing for you.

THE SUBZIWALLAH

Venkata Subramanian

RP Hall, 1995
eFarm (Founder and Managing Director)

---

eFarm, as Venkata Subramanian himself describes it, is 'Wal-Mart+eBay+dabbawallah' for the agriculture industry all processed and packaged into one business.

eFarm aims at providing the much-needed stability in a sector which is otherwise backward in terms of technology, and volatile for everyone involved in the chain. It gives the destitute farmer a glimmer of hope of becoming self-sufficient, and not merely depending on government subsidies and loan waivers for survival.

VENKY, AFTER COMPLETING his BArch from IIT Kharagpur in 1995, decided to pursue a career in IT. He worked for giants such as Satyam and Wipro for twelve years, where he held the position of Program Manager. In the meantime, he also completed his MS from the State University of New York, Albany, in 2003.

After all the years of hard work, it dawned on him that he was not doing anything productive with his life. He felt that he had given everything he had to offer to the IT industry, and wanted to do something of his own for a change.

Venky wanted to shatter the stereotypical notions of accumulating degrees in India. '**It's a set pattern which is followed and even if you don't follow it, your peer group forces you to do so.**' Moreover, he felt that entrepreneurship is not given importance in the country, and that in India, engineers are seen purely as job seekers, and therefore don't receive any backing when they want to start a business.

According to Venky, it is only the IT industry which has truly prospered in the country. Most of the upcoming businesses in India are in the IT and ITES sectors. But there is nothing innovative about it. What the IT industry has so far done here is to simply provide cheap service. If there is a job worth $45, it is done for a nominal $5 in the country. The whole IT industry is caught up in outsourcing as it provides them with quick money. Value creation after fifteen to twenty years of the IT industry, sadly, amounts to nothing.

If Venky wanted he could have easily joined another company and become its vice president. However, he felt he was running around in circles at an increasing speed and achieving nothing fruitful. According to him, it is essential to go through the rigours of corporate life to become a successful entrepreneur as it acquaints one with various facets of conducting a business. Moreover, Venky and his wife Srivalli had both lived the corporate life. They had seen many marital relationships turn sour in such a scenario. So, they decided to work on a new venture together.

After leaving his job, Venky decided to take a much deserved sabbatical. The time at his disposal was spent meeting up with friends who were successfully running their own businesses. At the same time, Venky decided to put the fair bit of land that he owned to use. He decided to grow fruits and vegetables on it. Some of his friends from the same industry were already selling fruits and vegetables to supermarkets like Spencer, so he was able to sell his produce through them. It was only after he had physically bought, sold, and delivered the goods that he realized the enormous potential of this sector.

As payments started to trickle in, Venky realized that the retail brands which he once considered big were, in reality, really small. He believes that it's not the local vendors who suffer due to the recession but the big players. The big retail stores operate their front-end stores at premium locations in the cities ending up with huge overhead costs, while the local vendors, the prime competition, operate in the interior pockets of the city, selling in garages and extensions of houses, thus making their space value negligible. As a result, they are able to make higher margins than the 'big retail shops'. Moreover, people are reluctant to visit these stores because of issues like non-availability of parking space, long queues for billing, and having to deal with untrained personnel.

Venky feels that there is a huge difference between Indian and American retail chains. According to him, Indian retailers have clearly misunderstood the functioning of American retails. Take Wal-Mart, where the emphasis is on the establishment of supply chains rather than front-end stores. In contrast, Indian chains focus more on opening stores in prime locations. This is a big misconception as far as the success of retail shops is concerned. Venky figured that the key to being successful in India was to do something economical but in a large volume.

After understanding the consumer dynamics of the agriculture industry, Venky turned his attention to production. He realized that the problem with agriculture in India was not at the primary level of farming as the production and its subsequent yield was high. The actual problem was in marketing. He found that farmers were paid too low a price for their produce.

Venky realized that the whole supply chain required overhauling to bring about some much-needed structure to the unorganized sector. He reasoned that farmers who don't get money from retailers go back to the mandi. This happens because the big brands fail to respect the importance of supply chains or link the consumer and producer in the right way.

The major problem with the agriculture industry is its lack of coordinated effort. There is not a single company in the market that can claim to have a holistic approach towards agriculture. It is only a select few companies that deal with things like agricultural tools, fertilizers, and pesticides. 'The reason behind this is that the industry itself is too big to handle, as it caters to 800 million people. Also, banks refrain from lending them money because the agriculture industry is unreliable and has insufficient data.'

What Venky came to realize is that ultimately it is the illiterate farmers in India who manage agriculture in their own crude ways. They are told to use 'drip irrigation' or 'high yielding variety seeds', procedures and techniques which require adequate technological training and knowledge for correct implementation. However, the educated person chooses to just dump knowledge on to the farmer. Venky is of the belief that farmers don't need money, all they require is proper training. The inappropriate use of new techniques doesn't increase yield; farmers are not getting any richer but only losing more money. Hence, over time, they are forced to sell their land to make some money out of it.

From his study of the agricultural sector, Venky concluded that people neither understood rural India nor did they care about it. The only people working for rural India are the NGOs. However, the problem Venky found with them was that they tend to be more passionate and emotional and less business minded. Their contribution to community development is immense, but at the end of the day it really comes down to work, money, selling, and marketing. Most NGOs find it almost impossible to be detached and do business with farmers in an objective fashion.

Venky started eFarm to provide the necessary treatment to an ailing agriculture industry. For that he created this company as a social enterprise. The objective is to reach out to the farmers, talk to them, and discuss their needs in order to provide them with the best possible solution.

The biggest challenge he faced was to work with farmers who still practised age-old methods of farming and had no knowledge of technological advancement. '**In every industry, the price is set first by demand and supply factors and it is then worked backwards to get the product ready at a price which is profitable to the producer. However, in agriculture, the market sets the price for you after you have the produce. A tomato seller taking his tomatoes to the mandi and asking for a price is plain foolishness. Farmers accuse middlemen of making money, but the process is such that it allows them to do so,**' says Venky.

eFarm was started to address these very issues. It started off by working on a 'supplier to customer' process. The method adopted by Venky was to predict the quantity and the variety of goods the consumer wanted and then procure those requirements. However, the question was how to predict these requirements. One could never speak to the end customers, as they would give a range of expectations, thus making an accurate prediction impossible. Instead, eFarm spoke to local vendors who had been operating in the market for years and had a fixed customer base. Hence, these vendors were more than capable of predicting how much they were going to sell and what their customers specifically wanted. eFarm began supplying to these vendors directly.

The general feeling among people is that street vendors do not sell in an optimized way. This, however, is a misconception. On the contrary, these vendors are shrewd operators. They buy a good mix of both premium and cheap goods in a way to satisfy all customer types. Through years of experience, they are able to predict the quantity that each product is going to sell. For instance, during festivals, vendors sell particular items which do not sell at other times. Thus they are sold at a particular price which consumers can't bargain. Nearly 95 percent of fruits and vegetables are sold by street vendors and not retail stores. So, it was imperative for Venky's company to work with this section in order to have a stable business set-up.

eFarm put the street vendors in groups of about 250. It started to take orders from these groups and amassed a bulk order, which was reasonable for both the farmers and them. The vendors were happy as they were able to get good quality products at cheaper prices. By taking bulk orders, eFarm was able to gauge the products that were in demand and estimate the time period of the demand for each product.

Venky got the farmers to sell him the produce in bulk, which could be pushed through to the slums. '**People are taken aback when I talk to them about the importance of slums. For me they are my premium customers—they pay the highest price for the poorest quality.**' Venky reasons that slum dwellers cannot afford to buy vegetables at high prices during the daytime, when it's mostly the middle class families who shop. The middle class families are very cautious about the quality of the food they buy, so they buy the best quality of fruits and vegetables. Slum dwellers get to buy only leftovers, sold at cheaper, flat prices during the evenings as they don't have any other option. And so it really is the evening markets where the real margins are earned.

After successfully setting up a distribution network among local vendors, eFarm turned its attention to the mid-end group—the more affluent people who are very particular about quality and pricing. This was achieved by tying up with vendors who catered to this section of people.

When eFarm was able to fulfil the needs of its mid-end customers, it started taking orders from large groups of apartments and individual customers like hospitals, canteens, and college hostels. These groups are highly predictable in nature as their menus are fixed. eFarm created a database of farmers on the one hand and customers on the other.

All that was required was to mix and match the quality as required by the vendors and other consumers, and market the goods accordingly.

eFarm, taking inspiration from the famed dabbawallahs of Mumbai, has set up clusters of collection centres in villages and distribution centres in cities to serve all the regions strategically. The prime difference between FedEx and the dabbawallahs is that FedEx has everything centralized. This concept cannot work in a country like India. The dabbawallahs have a decentralized model, which is highly efficient for India. If one surveys an area of a city, you will find a slum, a posh pocket, schools, colleges, and hotels. It's impossible to centrally demarcate an entire city into a slum, middle class, or posh area. Hence, to cater to each area of the city strategically, one needs to have distribution centres all over the city.

In a nutshell, eFarm recognized that in the existing agri-business scenario, it was the middlemen involved in the supply chain that were making it extremely inefficient, making neither the producer nor the consumer happy. eFarm has attempted to shrink this middle route, bringing the producer and consumer closer to each other.

The story behind how the company got its name is equally interesting. Venky says that the original idea was to start something like eBay for farmers, where they would be able to sell their produce on an auction basis. However, he soon realized that this model wasn't feasible, as the Internet had not really penetrated the interiors of the country. In India, people are more comfortable on the phone as they feel some kind of physical connectivity. Hence, the trust factor is more. The problem also lies in settlement and distribution. 'So if someone sitting in Chennai orders tomatoes and a farmer in Ooty has the supply for it, the match is made, but no assurance can be made for quality. Moreover, agriculture involves so much complexity that an automated process is not possible. A call centre is a much more feasible solution,' says Venky.

He feels that many of the tech entrepreneurs are great at innovations but not so good when it comes to business. 'They think by merely providing the technology they have solved the problem. There have been classic examples where the web portals have fired blanks. The technology needs to be user friendly. As an example, if you take the mobile phone, everyone wants one. Even the illiterates learn to use it because they want to. Hence, mobile phones are much better instruments for delivery to a larger base in India than web portals, which tech entrepreneurs have failed to recognize.' He also feels many of these tech entrepreneurs ignore the importance of things like marketing, pitching, finance, and customer relationship, which comes as a package with innovation. Ignorance in these areas can prove fatal.

The company has since taken up many consulting assignments related to agribusiness and management. In order to make others aware about real issues, it has started training sessions, workshops, and counselling sessions to give people the

---

EFARM'S ACHIEVEMENTS

Since its establishment, eFarm has won a number
of accolades, including a nomination at Tata NEN
Hottest Start-ups. Additionally, the Government of
India's Department of Science and Technology and
ICRISAT, Hyderabad, have chosen eFarm for a TePP
(Technopreneurs Promotion Programme) grant, while
also offering it incubation facilities.

---

right knowledge for operating in the agricultural sector. eFarm
has also undertaken a social initiative named 'RampUp', which
aims to promote the interests of disabled people. It has teamed
up with social service organizations to make the disabled feel
that they are no different from others. This will discourage
them from feeling sorry and, instead, help them become active
members of society. Venky himself ensures employment of
disabled persons in his company with the aim of showing them
that they can work just like any other person.

Venky feels that investors do not look at the calibre of the
people running the business, and judge them unfairly on the
basis of their balance sheets. They seem to care less for the ability
and domain knowledge of the entrepreneur. '**The reality is that
investors are scared to venture into unknown territories such
as agricultural and social businesses**,' he says.

But a chance meeting with Mumbai Angels, a leading
seed stage investment group based in Mumbai, got them
their first professional investors. Besides the money, they also

understood the business model well, and hence were able to correctly understand that even a social enterprise could be financially viable and replicate the scale of any other venture.

Through eFarm, Venky has been able to strike the right balance between a social initiative and an enterprise. As Venky puts it, '**Social entrepreneurship needs to have a delicate balance; if it's too social, you will be called an activist, and if it's too business oriented then you lose the essence of the enterprise.**' While it would be too much to expect one player to overhaul the entire agribusiness sector, it should definitely inspire other entrepreneurs to attempt to create more socially responsible enterprises in this and other ailing sectors in India. Venky epitomizes an entrepreneur sensitive to the needs of the time, displaying a willingness to plunge in and create solutions to existing problems. The effort he has shown should be reproduced by other entrepreneurs to create more socially responsible enterprises.

VENKY'S SUCCESS TIPS

- There is no sector in which you cannot work because of your lack of knowledge about it. Fundamental to starting up is applying yourself to it, doing the necessary groundwork.

- You need to have an interest and passion in the industry you are working in, in order to make a difference.

- Think long term; you should not let your investors drive your business. A lot of people have the tendency of working for three to four years and then exiting the company.

- Anyone else can have the same idea but what you bring to the table is your passion, dedication, and ability to learn and adapt. There will always be competition; you have to find a niche for yourself.

- You have to counsel yourself to not get bored or feel dejected at any point of time.

- Run your business within the scope of funds you have. Prove that you can sustain yourself at such a small level. That is your real test.

THE CYBER GUARDIAN

Bikash Barai

RK Hall, 2005
iViz TechnoSolutions
(Co-founder and CEO)

Bikash teamed up with fellow batchmate Nilanjan De to create iViz TechnoSolutions in the year 2005. At iViz, Bikash and Nilanjan developed a revolutionary technology capable of determining threats in a computer network. The tool finds all possible paths through which a computer can be attacked and comes up with viable solutions for the same.

Since then iViz has cemented its place in the global market as one of the most reputed computer network security companies.

BIKASH BARAI GREW UP in a typical lower-middle class Bengali family in Bandel, a small town near Kolkata. His father worked with the Hydrographic Survey of India, while his mother was a homemaker. Bikash was drawn to mathematics and physics, reading books on quantum mechanics and relativity with much interest, as early as Class 6, even though he understood little of it. The books were procured from people who used to recycle them into paper bags for Rs 15 a kg!

He joined IIT Kharagpur in 2000 to study a dual MTech degree in Computer Science and Engineering. Bikash flourished in the IIT environment, and took an active interest in campus life at the institute. He cleverly escaped the rigours of ragging by doing a magic show for the first time on Teacher's Day in front of thousands of people. He went on to help Kharagpur win the Inter IIT social and cultural competition, which was held only once in the history of the institute.

Apart from physics, Bikash had another love—painting. This made him participate in a lot of art and craft events in Kharagpur. He was so interested in art that he even completed a minor in Architecture. His mother fondly recounts how, when barely 5 or 6 years old, he visited an art teacher's house and asked to be taught. Even today, he pursues the hobby whenever he can sneak out a little time from work.

It was this very hobby that led to his first venture, a web portal dedicated to Indian paintings and art forms. Named 'bestfromIndia.com', it was floated in partnership with one other person in the year 2002. The portal was an instant success. It was ranked number one in any search related to Indian art forms on Google. The site was able to sell many paintings of Indian artists of repute besides some of his. This was done in collaboration with art galleries supplying collections of paintings by Jamini Roy and M.F. Husain, to name a few.

However, Bikash chose to discontinue the venture because even though it was a success, its operations were conducted on a very minuscule scale. The portal had been started more for philanthropic reasons than for moneymaking, and Bikash was able to perceive that it would not be sustainable in the longer run. He decided to move on.

It was during this time that he approached his batchmate Nilanjan De (the current CTO of iViz), who resided in the same hostel as him, for collaborating on a possible venture on ethical hacking. This was a topic that had lately occupied the minds of the IT industry. Nilanjan was a brilliant hacker who knew every person in the campus by their internet protocol address. Bikash had thought of creating a tool based on artificial intelligence (AI), which would simulate a human hacker. Even though Nilanjan knew little about the business, he worked without any inhibition.

Nilanjan taught Bikash how to hack a system, while Bikash automated the process. This was their initial mode of working till about 2004—both worked together and conducted research rather than ran a company. After obtaining their respective degrees, they chose to stay back on campus to develop the product. iViz was finally incorporated in 2005, though it really started to work as a company in mid-2006. The company was named iViz for 'Intelligent Vision', even though they themselves lacked a clear vision, making the name very generic. In spite of conducting the required research and being equipped with the right technology, they didn't have a final product to sell to their customers. They wanted to do something in the area of security, hacking, and penetration testing, but there was no structure to it. What they thought would work at that time, didn't.

In spite—or even because—of this, the duo received tremendous motivation and support from fellow IITians and professors. Incubation in IIT had not been formalized at the time and whatever support they received was from professors like A. Gupta and P.P. Chakrabarti who helped them with their research work, apart from guiding them on company strategy and in matters related to technology.

However, Bikash's parents were not very comfortable with the idea of him starting his own business. One relative even went on to remark to his mother, '*Bikash computerey dokaan khulechey*' (Bikash has opened up a computer shop). His mother was expectedly petrified, begging him to take up a job, but Bikash was determined and worried little about his mother's concerns as he knew she would accept his decision later.

It required a lot of willpower on Bikash's part to jump straight into the boots of an entrepreneur in his undergraduate years. He didn't have the perfect plan initially, as he believed that for being an entrepreneur no plan B was required. The absence of an alternative plan paves the way for the learning process where one gradually figures it all out. '**Getting into entrepreneurship is not something you can first learn in some classroom simulation and then practise the real thing outside. You have to practise it and learn things at the same time,**' he says. However, Bikash does feel that once you have been at a place like IIT, you feel confident that you will end up doing something worthwhile in your life.

One year into the business, Bikash and Nilanjan sought to employ a person who would look after team management. While their friends were getting placed, they went to Kolkata to recruit a few management students. On reaching Kolkata, they got on a bus to go to the management school only to realize midway that going by taxi would reflect better on both them and their company. So they got off the bus about a kilometre before their destination and hired a cab from there. Placements at IIT, in those days, was a fashionable affair. As Bikash vividly remembers, one company even had a Miss Bangalore runner-up accompany them for their pre-placement talk. And Bikash's company was anything but fashionable. They made their presentation without a laptop; numerous people were interviewed, and the job was offered to three, but only one of the potential candidates joined. That one person still works for the company.

In 2005, iViz raised a formidable amount of Rs 1.5 crore from US-based eRevMax Technologies, after which the company migrated to Kolkata. eRevMax (a leader in revenue management system for the online hotel industry) initially gave them $1000 for their pilot project, but the company was so taken up with their technology that they finally ended up being iViz's angel investor.

Until then, iViz had mainly concentrated on automated penetration testing, which involved analysing the security of a computer or a series of network computers by simulating an attack on the system. Every computer has a firewall on its gateway that determines the security strength of the system. While hacking, the hacker tries to breach this firewall and gain access to the data contained in the system. Penetration testing can determine whether a system is secure or not.

It took a while before they could attain their Eureka moment: They were doing a penetration test for an organization, skilfully breaking into all parts of the network; they got the password of the CEO and broke into all the email accounts. They then presented their report to the client. While writing the report, it occurred to them that penetration could have been carried out in a different manner. So a request was made to allow them to carry out penetration once again. On being given the chance, they tried it the different way and it worked. That was when it dawned upon them that the best hackers in the world had numerous pathways at their disposal if they were to break into the system, just like the two they had discovered. This necessitated the need for customers to know all possible paths through which their system could be broken into, so that their system is completely secure.

The big question staring them in their faces was whether they had it in them to build a tool which could simulate all possible attack paths. There are certain problems and programs which, even if fed into a supercomputer, would take hundreds of years to solve. This was precisely one of the problems which, they realized, could not be solved by conventional AI methods. Since they had done a lot of practical hacking, they were quick to realize that many of the theoretical possibilities were redundant. After removing these very possibilities, their problem became much simpler to solve. The product was eventually launched in 2007 keeping these factors in mind.

The challenge, however, was anything but over. Bikash found that the product was not easy to use, and only an expert in network security could make much of it. He realized that customers wanted a usable tool as a solution to their problems and not an advanced technology that handicapped them. Hence, he decided to migrate to the Software as a Service (SaaS) model.

iViz made the product on demand, becoming the first company to start 'on-demand' penetration testing. Bikash realized that through direct selling, his per customer revenue was not as high as he had expected. So, in order to boost revenue, iViz entered into partnerships with the best computer security companies in the world.

Bikash remembers his growth fundraising experience as a mixed yet very important one. He now clearly understands how to approach venture capitalists, present a business plan to them, and how to seal the right deal. Bikash remembers how one of the VC firm's partners came to his set-up to have a look at the organization. He liked it and was ready to invest in the company. Bikash was invited to Bengaluru where he met the limited partners; they, however, required a detailed business plan. It took them a few months to get the plan ready but by the time they showed it to him, he had already forgotten about their business model, and his interest level had diminished. They realized that all big deals should be closed immediately, because a delay might lead to an afterthought, and VCs don't have a great attention span. This experience proved to be only a minor setback for Bikash, as iViz later got offers from three other VCs, the most notable of which was from IDG Ventures from whom they received a funding of $2.5 million.

The story of iViz is one of constant transitions. One starts with an idea and by the time it works, it is completely different from the initial model. Bikash and Nilanjan, too, started with a service, built a product, and finally developed a SaaS model. They changed their model as per the requirement of the market, a crucial ingredient for their success. Bikash believes that one should not be married to an idea as it can prove to be highly dangerous. Becoming dispassionate with the idea is necessary as it gives a different vantage point. In the course of running the company, Bikash's thought process itself underwent a sea change as well. When one starts a company, one claims full ownership of it. Then, when one raises money, the company becomes a distinct member in its own right, separate from its owner. Bikash runs his company like any other big corporate house, with a board at the helm. An investor expects that kind of corporate governance from a company of some repute.

IVIZ'S ACHIEVEMENTS

Many honours have been bestowed upon iViz Security since its establishment. The company was in the shortlist of the world's top eight contenders at the Intel-UC Berkeley Technology Entrepreneurship Challenge in 2006. It was recognized as one of the top six security companies in the world by the US Department of Homeland Security, London Business School, and US Navy, besides being the Red Herring Top 100 Asia winner in 2008. NASSCOM selected iViz as one of the top four emerging product companies in 2008 while *Business Today* hailed it as one of the ten hottest start-ups the very same year.

Throughout the company's journey, right from ideation to execution, Bikash learnt many important lessons about running a successful organization. One of these was that ideators may get excited by new ideas and technology, even though it might not appeal to the customer. Until the customer's basic needs are addressed, he/she would never purchase the idea. When Bikash started off, he realized that customers were not concerned about the security of the system but about the business continuity, brand, and compliance. This was a big realization, and they repositioned their product based on this revelation. The implementation of an idea was a huge lesson from this.

Another lesson he learnt in the process was about team composition. He realized that having the right set of people in the team is critical for the business. The initial failures of the company were a result of having like-minded people in the team, and not people with a complementary set of skills. This lasted for a short period of time, after which Bikash tried to gather the best people from all over the world to work for the company in order to create some sort of balance.

Today, iViz has offices in Boston, USA, London, UK, and Bengaluru, and twenty other countries in the world. Within four years of its existence, iViz has had an exponential growth. It is one of the hottest IT start-ups in India, having received rave reviews not only in the national market but all over the globe. iViz is expected to become a $30 million to $40 million company in the coming few years, a pioneer in the field of on-demand security.

The world can rest assured that iViz is going to help it stay one step ahead of the hackers.

BIKASH'S SUCCESS TIPS

- While starting up, focus on one idea by eliminating other choices. Choose one thing and do it right. Keeping too many options open will lead you nowhere.

- Another important thing required while starting up is passion. Don't let your lack of business knowledge restrict you.

A RESOLVE TO SUCCEED

Vikram Kumar

Patel Hall, 2006
Dataresolve Technologies
(Founder and CEO)

Ever since Vikram's third year at IIT, he wanted to create a technology that would transform the world. What differentiated him from most of the other IITians who have similar dreams was the fact that he believed in them. The power of his belief gave him the tenacity and determination required to establish a successful venture from scratch.

Dataresolve is one of those Indian IT companies which is gradually changing the global perception of the Indian IT industry—a hotbed for ground-breaking technologies.

IT WAS IN HIS SECOND YEAR AT IIT, while working on a project under Professor R.N. Banerjee that Vikram started to dabble in writing computer programs. All around him start-ups from the institute were flourishing, and Vikram and his friends felt that they too could make something of it. However, it turned out to be nothing more than wishful thinking on the part of most of his batchmates. IIT saw many MNCs snap up the students with cushy corporate jobs and high pay packages. Vikram too unwillingly went through the placement process, and was hired by one of the MNCs. Professor R.N. Banerjee, however, told him to stay back with the promise he would help Vikram to start his own company while working on some of his projects. Vikram had nothing to lose as Professor Banerjee was paying him a decent salary, so he decided to stay back. However, nothing materialized out of this arrangement.

While working on his business plan for an endpoint security company, Vikram was asked by a senior who was running a successful company which was already funded to come and join him. Vikram was wary of the offer as he was certain about his dream of starting his own company. His senior told Vikram that his company was small with just five to six people working in it, and it would be the same as working in a start-up. Vikram decided to join him.

The Universal Serial Bus (USB) had just made an appearance in the market and was taking off in a huge way. The USB was designed to standardize the connection of computer peripherals, such as keyboards, pointing devices, digital cameras, printers, portable media players, disk drives, and network adapters to PCs, both to communicate and to supply electric power. It has become commonplace on other devices, such as smartphones, PDAs, and video game consoles. The USB has effectively replaced a variety of earlier interfaces, such as serial and parallel ports, as well as separate power chargers for portable devices. Till 2008, about 2 billion USB devices were sold each year, and approximately 6 billion devices were sold in total.

The USB, coupled with the emergence of devices like smartphones, was making the storage and transfer of data easy as pie. However, along with the USB came the threat of network security. Data could now be transferred freely and easily, and hacking became rampant. There was no one making computers secure against these types of transfers. The company that Vikram joined dealt with network security of computers to minimize hacking. And he began to form some ideas of his own. Vikram could see the scope for developing a security software in this field. After more in-depth research, Vikram came to learn that this was a standard threat known as Data Loss Prevention (DLP), and two to three companies were already working to make the computer more secure. Vikram knew he was on to something big. On the other hand, the company that Vikram was working for was growing extremely fast and was about to raise its second round of funding a few months after Vikram had joined. Vikram felt that he had not contributed substantially to the success of the company, and didn't think that he had much to contribute. He decided to quit and start his own.

However, if wishes were horses, beggars would ride. Vikram had no idea about how to start a company. He haunted the IT hub in Salt Lake, Kolkata, meeting CEOs of various companies. They met him mainly because he was from IIT and so he might have some great product to offer them. But nothing came from those meetings. Vikram realized that he needed a business plan. He stayed home for a week, searched the web, and put one together.

He started to meet people again, but it was to no avail. Then, one day, he happened to meet Kaustav Ghosh, an entrepreneur and Vice President of Connectiva Systems, who immediately took an interest in Vikram's idea. He gave Vikram some solid advice—to sell his idea, he needed to make the perfect business plan. Fifty versions later, Vikram was ready to meet Kaustav Ghosh again. He asked Vikram how much capital he required, and Vikram gave him a rough estimate.

However, the money wasn't enough. Vikram was already in debt; his credit card had shot its limit and he had no liquid cash available. He couldn't pay his rent or buy credit on his phone. He didn't even have enough money for his day-to-day living expenses. Any other person would have thrown in the towel and quit the idea of starting a company when faced with such financial troubles, but Vikram was determined. There was no question of turning back from the road he'd chosen. What Vikram did next was make one of the smartest moves, one that got him back on track. In 2008, he decided to move back to IIT Kharagpur and set up an office space there. It was a good decision as he could live in the hostel and have food on credit by eating in the canteen.

Vikram was allotted an office space in the Science Technology and Entrepreneurs Park (STEP) and started his company Dataresolve Technologies. In the meantime, Devesh Mittal (current CTO of Dataresolve Technologies), Vikram's previous hostel mate, had left his plush job at British Telecom to join Vikram. Together, they hired a few students from IIT. The company also procured Rs 10 lakh from the entrepreneurial support provided by IIT in the form of Technology Incubation and Entrepreneurial Training Society (TIETS) funds. This was a phenomenal breakthrough for Vikram. After receiving the funds they started working on their first product, which they completed in seven months. They called the product Uhook. Uhook was designed to help users protect their personal and confidential data on their computers from unauthorized access or from being copied through removable devices like USBs, digital cameras, iPods, cell phones, etc. They released it on the Web and it was instantly sold. It might seem like a small thing, but it gave their small venture a boost. They continued to work on new products and in some time acquired four genuine customers.

In April 2009, after getting the much-needed stability, Vikram decided to move back to Kolkata. Relocating to Kolkata was very good for business. They got their first deal with a company just a few months later. Prior to that, they'd had customers who had bought Dataresolve's products for personal use only. It was perhaps the toughest job they ever had to do. Their client's office was in a village 32 kilometres away from Kolkata, where Vikram was based. So, if there were any software malfunctions, the client would not be able to access the files and applications on their systems, thus bringing their work to a complete standstill. Vikram and his team would have to rush to the client's office during such circumstances. They had to make at least fourteen to fifteen trips before they were able to make the final version stable. This experience was crucial for them as they were able to test the product in real time. They were now equipped to handle any problems that could arise.

Despite acquiring many customers Dataresolve was not able to become financially self-sufficient. In November 2009, they were out of money, and were on the verge of shutting shop. However, Vikram's never-say-die spirit helped them stay afloat. He was able to convince his mentor, Kaustav Ghosh, to loan him some money to keep the company's head above water.

Vikram firmly believes that Dataresolve has much more to offer people than its competitors, as its technology is far superior. The other DLP companies had adopted the

---

DATARESOLVE'S ACHIEVEMENTS

The first online data security product that Dataresolve launched, in May 2009, was graded among the best security products by *PC Quest*, with the free version having a user base of more than 20,000 people. Since its inception, the company has been able to garner forty-four customers in more than a dozen countries. It also boasts of more than 100 affiliates and partners worldwide.

---

content analysis method in which the software analyses the data and classifies it as confidential or non-confidential. So, whatever has been marked as confidential is not allowed to be transferred without the permission of the user. Vikram found this model genuinely flawed because confidentiality might change with passage of time; what is not confidential today might be confidential tomorrow. Content analysis is not able to assess this. The second reason was that the content analysis method is not always 100 percent accurate. What Dataresolve did differently was to make a flexible product where the users themselves can mark any number of files or folders on their computer system which they think are personal or confidential. Dataresolve's product secures these marked items against theft or any virus that can corrupt files and folders. Only if their customer asks for content analysis do they do it.

The other problem that DLP companies faced was the boom of access devices such as iPhones, iPads, etc. If one made

241

security products only for Windows and Linux, it wouldn't cover other products. Dataresolve designed its product in such a way that it could provide protection across multiple operating systems in the long run. These features are quite handy for clients as they can sit in an office in Mumbai and monitor the data transfer activities of all their offices around the world. It is also quite useful in parental control on the activities of their children. The parents can use Dataresolve's product to get a complete list of all their children's activities on the computer. If they find some unwanted activity, they can block them. It can be used as a foolproof protection by big organizations against data theft and whistle-blowing agencies like Wikileaks.

Dataresolve got lucky because of the time they entered the market. It started out when the evolution of DLP had already ended. Hence, it was in a better position to weigh the pros and cons of the products that were already available. Dataresolve's competitors, despite knowing that their products had failed, couldn't do anything. The competitors already had a 2 to 3 million consumer base, which they were serving using the content analysis paradigm. If they decided to shift from content analysis, it would cost them huge amounts of time and money.

By the start of 2010, Vikram felt that in order to expand his business and negate the disadvantage of being an Indian technology start-up he would require more funds. Fund-raising was one of the most essential lessons Vikram learnt in his entrepreneurial journey. He was able to realize the actual picture of the Indian seed funding scenario. He must have approached about thirty investors, out of which 90 percent were absolutely bogus. They had no money to invest but were posing as VCs to get their hands on a good business plan or idea. There were only three to four genuine investors; and interacting with them was beneficial for Dataresolve. However, a few of them didn't want to invest and Vikram was not comfortable with the terms and conditions of the others who wanted to. Despite all this, Dataresolve was able to secure funds by May 2010 by settling on the option of multiple investors.

Vikram feels that one of the biggest concerns for a start-up is having a stable team. The success of a company has a lot to do with the team it builds. Vikram has concentrated on quality rather than quantity when it comes to his team. Dataresolve consists of six members, all of whom are from IIT Kharagpur.

VIKRAM'S TAKE ON THE TEAM

'When you are starting a company, you have to be honest and candid with the people working with you. With this approach, they might not commit to you, but if you try to hide something, it will prove harmful to the company. We have a small but stable team now, who deliver their best for the company.'

In the distant future, Vikram wants to build the best technology in his domain of expertise. In other words, if anyone buys a laptop or any other system, he or she should know that Dataresolve is around to secure their data!

Vikram is a perfect role model for all students who dare to dive in the ocean of entrepreneurship instead of taking up a cosy job after graduation. He and his team have proved that a group of fresh Indian graduates can create a high-end technology product right here in India.

VIKRAM'S SUCCESS TIPS

- Go for a regular job only if you're a hundred percent sure that's what you really want to do. Otherwise, start a company. It is quite easy; all you need is dedication and some amount of patience.

- If you want a small amount of money for starting up, get it through an investor with the help of some personal contact. If you are able to find some institutional investor like I did in IIT Kharagpur, then there is nothing like it.

- Beware of some investors in India. All they do is kill your time and motivation. They convince you that your business will fail. Go to investors who have actually funded start-ups.

- Don't make a business plan just for the sake of making it. Visualize your company and put your heart and soul in it.

- For raising money, you do need a good B-plan and presentation skills, but all that is secondary. The most important thing is that you have to convince the investor that you can make money.

RIDING ON CLOUD NINE

Krishna Mehra

RK Hall, 2006
Capillary Technologies
(Co-founder and CTO)

What happens when a smart mind meets smart business acumen? The result is Krishna Mehra. Krishna heads Capillary Technologies, a company which, in the words of the high profile investor and head of Google India Rajan Anandan, 'will become one of India's most valuable technology companies over the coming years'. This, about a company barely three years old.

KRISHNA MEHRA, ACCORDING to his batchmates at IIT Kharagpur, was a prodigy and destined for great things in life. He was an all-rounder, excelling in both studies and extra-curricular activities. Krishna's first brush with entrepreneurship was during his time at IIT itself. Krishna and Aneesh Reddy (Co-founder and CEO of Capillary Technologies) had started the Entrepreneurship Cell at IIT Kharagpur to help other start-ups springing up in the institute. In his final year, Krishna was working with Minekey, a start-up at IIT Kharagpur. This was a very important experience for him as he learnt about the nuances of work, what tools to use, and what one should focus on in a technology company. Soon after he graduated, Minekey raised $3 million from New Enterprise Associates (NEA), which was a huge confidence booster for him.

Krishna graduated with top honours from IIT Kharagpur. He decided to join Microsoft Research in Bengaluru after his graduation. At Microsoft, Krishna was able to further enrich his understanding of technology and he also learnt how to work in a more professional environment. By the time he left Microsoft, he had six patents and seven international conference papers to his name.

Krishna had been working at Microsoft Research for two years, but was keen on starting something of his own.

He met his friend from RK Hall, Aneesh, a day after his birthday in 2008. Aneesh was a mechanical engineer, who was then working at ITC. They were both eager to plunge into entrepreneurship. They thought that the mobile and retail sectors were taking off in India and it made sense to explore opportunities in these sectors. The first idea that they had was to offer local discount deals to users through their mobile phones. They called it Deal Hunt. '**If I am a consumer staying in Koramangala, Bengaluru, and wish to find out the best deals, best offers, and best discounts nearby, I should be able to get them on my mobile. It sounded very interesting to us at that time and we decided to give it a shot.**'

They found out that the Technology Incubation and Entrepreneurial Training Society (TIETS) at IIT Kharagpur gave seed loans to both students and alumni for their ventures. Krishna moved to Kolkata from Bengaluru to join Aneesh. They concretized their idea, did the required research, and presented a business plan to the TIETS committee. Their product carried a fair bit of IP, which pleased the committee. The committee approved their project for the seed funding. Capillary Technologies was founded in August 2008 with a soft loan of Rs 15 lakh from TIETS. Just around that time, Ajay Modani, a junior to Krishna from IIT Kharagpur, joined them as one of the co-founders in the team.

As a simple and smart first thing to do, they decided to field-test their product. They started out with a few colleges. They were then handling regular stuff such as mobile registrations and other kinds of engagements at student festivals. After that they worked with the Kolkata police during Durga Puja. People would SMS them their location and they would reply whether there was a traffic jam in that location or not. Capillary did these events to learn and did not get paid for them at all. The idea was to see what the practical problems in deploying the product were, try different things, and see how the users responded, while getting some publicity.

Krishna and his team learnt a lot from these simple tests; most importantly, they learnt that people do not like to SMS a number to obtain some service. They also realized that for them to succeed with this model—of people using SMS for finding the best deals available—they would have to invest a whole lot more money in creating brand awareness, marketing and call centres than they had previously estimated.

Capillary decided to reposition its product. Traditionally, retailers hand out plastic loyalty cards to customers to monitor things like customer retention, and customers in return get discounts on their future purchase from the outlet. But there are a number of problems with plastic cards: they are unwieldy, cost a lot, and customers don't sign up for these cards, etc. Capillary came up with the idea of creating a very lightweight mobile program that could be used by retailers, sparing them the hassles related to loyalty cards. When they spoke to retailers about this, they realized that there was a lot of enthusiasm for this product.

So by December 2008, they started building the product, which was to provide a mobile solution in place of the inefficient loyalty cards. John Miller, an apparel retail brand, was the first to show interest in the product and Capillary got them the product by March 2009. They signed up Madura Garments and Peter England soon after.

The Capillary product was a simple but brilliant idea. They called it Intouch. It helped retailers serve their customers better through customer transaction data. If a customer bought something from a retail outlet and got it billed, his latest transaction with his name and mobile number would be captured by Intouch. This data would be analysed in real time, and immediately, a discount coupon would be forwarded to them via SMS. '**If you have bought two expensive shirts, Intouch would push a coupon to the customer saying: you are a valuable customer, and we are offering 15 percent discount on trousers today, only for you!**' Since the customer has just bought two shirts, buying another trouser at a discount makes for a good offer, especially as it's served instantly. The customer is already in the retail shop and can be tipped over for an impulse purchase.

The beauty of the analytics in a cloud-based system is that the data centre for storing and processing is located not in the shop but somewhere else, something similar to keeping your documents on Google's data centre so that it can be accessed from any other computer. This means minimum hassle for the retailer, who doesn't have to bother with data storage and maintenance and thus gets a high quality service for minimum investment. While previous programmes through loyalty cards typically took two–three years to ensure a tangible return on investment, cloud-based systems can exhibit an immediate increase in sales.

By June 2009, Capillary hired a few more people and became a seven-member team. They moved to Bengaluru as most of their then clients were based there. Initially, they made a three-bedroom house their headquarters. The transition wasn't smooth as the house didn't have any water during the day and even transportation from the place was difficult. Moreover, the economy was in the throes of recession. Eventually, they had to move once again to a better locality.

Being at the right place at the right time can sometimes be extremely crucial. One day Krishna went to the Open Coffee Club, an open and informal meeting place for people involved in start-ups in Bengaluru city, to find that the speaker that day was Karthee Madasamy of Qualcomm Ventures. Qualcomm was conducting the QPrize Business Plan competition and Karthee encouraged everyone to submit their plans. Krishna submitted their presentation at absolutely the last moment. Capillary made it to the shortlist of eight participants. The Capillary team was pleasantly surprised with this outcome. Having made it to the finals, Krishna thought they should put their best foot forward. The team then went ahead to make the final presentation. They were very anxious; to them the other participants seemed far more experienced. They never thought they even stood a chance of winning the event. The event was at Leela Palace, and the most they expected was to go to the event and enjoy a nice dinner. As Krishna recalls, they weren't even paying attention when the winner's name was announced. It took them a while to grasp that they had actually won the competition. Winning the Qualcomm QPrize gave a tremendous boost to their confidence. They received $100,000 in convertible notes funding. With this success in the bag and the buzz it created, they took the opportunity to raise some angel funding in January 2010.

Up till then Capillary had been dealing only in software, but this was the time when they hired Sridhar Bollam to help them start paying more and more attention to analytics. By the middle of 2010, Capillary had grown to a company of twenty-five to thirty people. With feedback, its product was getting into good shape, with the addition of new features and options. For example, its product initially didn't have a store module, but based on feedback, they developed it in the first one to two months. It's been their one killer tool for optimum return on investment. Similarly, they have added customer feedback system, promotional vouchers, etc.—all based on customer feedback.

This idea was easily customized to other sectors. For instance, in the case of food, Capillary focused on coupons which would get the customers to order food for a second time; in spas, the focus was on increase in retention and repeat visits; in supermarkets, the emphasis was on increasing the variety of goods sold—if a customer buys a certain kind of product he will be encouraged to buy from a different category of goods.

CAPILLARY TECHNOLOGIES' ACHIEVEMENTS

Capillary Technologies, which combines cloud computing, mobile phones, retail outlets, and customer relationship management (CRM) in a unique way, has seen a transaction throughout of $500 million (Rs 2309 crore) in 2011.

It works with more than 100 brands across more than 6000 stores, and reaches 15 million consumers. It is already India's largest brand loyalty provider and has expanded to markets in the UK, Middle East, Singapore, and South Africa. The company which went from twelve employees in August 2009 to 150 employees, is now targeting an incredible 8x growth in revenue in the year 2011. It is only three years old.

Capillary won the Qualcomm QPrize Business Competition in 2009, which brought investments from Qualcomm. It also won at Techsparks 2011, TieCon Entrepreneurial Excellence Awards 2011, and is on the NASSCOM Emerge League of Ten.

The product was by then recognized and doing well; customers were happy with the return on investment they were getting. Capillary got their first three clients in a year's time. This helped them establish case studies and consumer validation. Once their market study was established, the ease of product use, and a simple revenue model—charging a retailer per store per month—made the adoption easy. The next year they had thirty clients, and then usage exploded. Today, they have more than a hundred clients across 6000 stores, with 15 million customers registered. Some of the key deals they did during the initial days, according to Krishna, were with well-known brands such as Madura Garments, Indus League Clothing, and Raymond Limited, which made it much easier and faster to get new customers.

Krishna did not want to merely sit on Capillary's initial success in the Indian retail market and wanted to take the company overseas. Speaking to their customers made him and his team realize that it might actually make sense to explore international markets. They started talking with their contacts and recognized that their product seemed to be unique even in foreign markets. The product was also adaptable to a client overseas as the only changes required were to the user-side interfaces. The bigger challenge was to get the first client and build a network in that country. So the next step was to formulate a strategy for international expansion. Towards the end of December 2010, they made a couple of tours: Aneesh went to the UK and the US, and Krishna to Dubai. They tapped into some of their Indian retailer contacts who had subsidiaries abroad in the UK. Their conversations with the retailers there were very encouraging and they decided to aim for international growth to see whether they could actually sell the product in foreign markets. By April 2011, they had opened offices in London and Dubai.

Capillary has now grown to 150 people. They work to ensure that the processes are in place so that software quality and product quality is top notch; the analytics is powerful, and helps the retailers. Anticipating and reacting to market changes quickly has always been among the signature traits of leaders. Capillary Technologies has always been close to retailers, speaking to them, trying to understand their needs and requirements, and modifying the product accordingly. If a service is required and it is lacking in the product today, they provide it manually and later integrate it into the product.

As customer interactions are changing in the Facebook/Twitter world, Capillary has been working harder to keep its product up to date. Facebook keeps altering regularly, and by aligning to its changes they are able to give brands a robust proposition. Capillary got itself ISO certified to show clients that it is updated in terms of security and processes. In fact, it is the only company in this business space that has got itself an ISO 27001 certification. Big retail brands need to be comfortable with the security levels. Each client's data is maintained in silos as Capillary takes data security very seriously.

Krishna thinks their tremendous growth was also possible because of an unsettling change that has swept the world with respect to technology: mobile phones becoming a necessity, the wide availability of broadband connectivity, and thus the ability to connect systems easily.

One of the other company strengths is in its founders. Krishna knew Aneesh from their IIT days, so they had the right kind of comfort level working with each other. Aneesh joined ITC after graduating and Krishna joined Microsoft Research. So basically, Krishna comes from a software background while Aneesh comes from an operational background. Their skill sets are complementary, allowing them to focus on different things. Even while doing the same thing they come up with different ideas, so Capillary has had diversity of opinion, which has worked out very well for them. Both of them are good at networking and that helps in opening up a large network for them.

Krishna attributes a lot of his success to IIT Kharagpur. Getting funding from TIETS initially made all the difference, in his opinion. Though they managed their personal expenses through their own savings, they really needed that money to travel around, buy computers, etc. It made the difference between travelling by train versus travelling by air. For a start-up, time is of the utmost importance, being the scarcest resource, and with the TIETS money, they were able to buy time. It also created breathing space to operate with more freedom. They didn't spend a lot of money, but the funds created a comfort level that if anything went wrong, they could take care of it, thus giving them the freedom to try out different things.

Krishna believes that the outlook for technology companies in India is very bright. 'We now have a very strong talent

KRISHNA'S TAKE ON ENTREPRENEURSHIP

As for the ideal time for graduates to venture into entrepreneurship, Krishna believes that there is no black or white answer. Whether they should get some experience in the industry like he did depends entirely on the sector you enter into. Having experience definitely helps in understanding how company culture works, he believes, because it's completely different from the college culture.

pool. People are staying back in the country instead of going abroad. All the global biggies are set up here and have their research labs or development centres in India. So people are getting the right kind of training and are being empowered with the right tools to build big tech companies.' People are the most critical aspects of a start-up—both Krishna and Aneesh feel their people are their most important assets.

Krishna is very excited and upbeat about the future. 'We have practically managed to build a company as salesforce.com for retail CRM. This is now a platform that can be grown very rapidly. The core is already in place. We have managed to plug in a lot of different services into Capillary's cloud solution to the extent that a lot of other players now build on top of our systems and provide services to retailers, including creative agencies, reward management systems, social media management companies, etc. No other service comes close to what we provide. We have a very distinct and powerful value proposition for the retailers. We believe our product can be the next benchmark in customer engagement.'

Krishna is enjoying building his company, especially the fact that every day brings different things. 'On some days it is early morning flights and on other days there is late night rollout of new features—you are always up to something exciting!'

Now isn't that what entrepreneurship is all about?

KRISHNA'S SUCCESS TIPS

- In the beginning, focus on getting customers. Every small thing you do needs to be towards that goal.

- You need to set aggressive targets; you can't really wait for customers to come to you.

- Understand the market, build a network there, and be able to win clients. In the first two years of a start-up it is of utmost importance to gain traction, in users or customers.

ACKNOWLEDGEMENTS

First and foremost, we would like to thank all the entrepreneurs who took out invaluable time from their busy schedule for us.

We would like to thank Professor Dr Damodar Acharya, Director, IIT Kharagpur, for officially endorsing this book, and Dr Duvvuri Subbarao, Governor, Reserve Bank of India, and for giving us the confidence we needed.

A special thank you to Professor Amit Patra, Dean of Alumni Affairs, IIT Kharagpur, who was always full of encouragement about this project.

We are indebted to the IIT Kharagpur fraternity; and alumni such as Chinna Boddipalli and Professor P.P. Iyer, who have been very supportive in the fulfilment of our initiative. As members and alumni of the Entrepreneurship Cell, IIT Kharagpur, we are thankful to the organization for its assistance.

A big thank you to all our families, teachers, and friends, especially Ankur Kumar Agarwal, Sujana Mukherjee, Kushagra Udai, and Arpan Ganguli who helped us with invaluable feedback for some of the stories.

To Subhendu Panigrahi, who helped us during the inception of this book and the writing team of the Entrepreneurship Cell (Pradeep and Raunak). And a special thanks to Amit Haralalka for providing us with some sound advice.

We sincerely thank Kanishka Gupta at Writer's Side Agency for his help and guidance to us first-time authors in bringing this project to a successful and satisfying conclusion.

Finally, we thank our publishers Random House India for taking up this project, and our editors, Milee Ashwarya and Trisha Bora, for their invaluable inputs on the manuscript.